The **ORIGIN** of the **UNIVERSE**

Sherlie =
645 - 7620
Bill - 645 - 7304

The **ORIGIN** of the **UNIVERSE**

"...who stretchest out the heavens like a curtain:" Psalm 104:2

A
COMBINED
BIBLICAL
AND
SCIENTIFIC
PERSPECTIVE

E. a. Cooper

Emerson Cooper

Pleasant W rd

A Division of WINEPRESS PUBLISHING

Artwork: Cover: Jonny Ericson, Figure 6.2: David Richardson.

ISBN 1-4141-0025-6
Library of Congress Catalog Card Number: 2003110077

To Marjorie, Roslyn, Stephen and Margo who shared in my teaching ministry; to all my chemistry professors who nurtured my love for chemistry; and to the thousands of students who gave me the opportunity to learn in the process of teaching them.

Table of Contents

Foreword

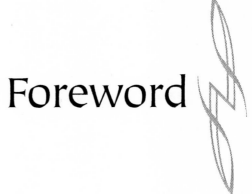

In this thoughtful and intellectually stimulating book, Emerson Cooper uses logical arguments to eloquently delineate his thoughts on the origin of the universe from "a combined biblical and scientific perspective." His approach helps the reader to understand the logic of a transcendent "Creator-God" as the originator and designer of the cosmos. Most scientists and theologians agree that the universe had a beginning. Emerson Cooper contends that one possible beginning can be explained by the big bang phenomenon where God is the initiator of the creation process.

As an addendum to Professor Cooper's excellent presentation, I would like to add the recently proposed expanding sheet theory. During the last two decades, Paul Steinhardt of Princeton and Neil Turok of Cambridge University suggested an alternative model to the big bang theory for the creation of the universe (http://www.sciencedaily.com/releases/2002/04/020429080540.htm). The details of their theory can be found in Appendix A of this book.

In addition to his excellent and elegant discussion of the origin of the universe from a combined biblical and scientific perspective, Professor Cooper also discusses two very important topics that lie at the interface of science and religion and are of the greatest interest to all persons interested in the subject of origins. Such topics as the age of the earth and the origin of life on planet earth are of paramount interest to all readers who are interested in knowing and understanding what science and the Bible have to say about these two important subjects. Professor Cooper concludes his book with a documented non-biblical essay on the question, Is macroevolution scientifically valid? This essay is an appeal to all those who have accepted macroevolution as a scientific fact without pausing to question its scientific validity. His presentation of "ten powerful scientific arguments against evolution and the testimonies of scientists" not only puts evolution on the defensive but also demolishes the whole super structure of this theory. In brief, his essay leads to the inescapable conclusion that macroevolution is indeed a theory without evidence.

David Richardson
Former Professor of Chemistry at Oakwood College
Huntsville, Alabama

Preface

Two Profound Questions

The two most profound questions that the human mind can contemplate are, "Does God exist?" and "What is the origin of the universe?" It is interesting to note that the book of Genesis begins with the answers to these two questions: "In the beginning God created the heaven and the earth." Genesis 1:1 affirms the existence of a transcendent God who created the universe. When Bertrand Russell, the agnostic English philosopher and mathematician, was asked the question, "Where did the universe come from?" the only response that he could give was, "The universe is just there." To acknowledge that the universe had a beginning is to acknowledge that there was a creation, which was brought about by a creator.

Concerning the origin of the universe, there are three possibilities. The first is that the universe has always existed. The second is that the universe created itself out of nothing. And the third is that the universe was created by a transcendent Creator-God. No other possibilities are known. The first possibility can be dismissed because the Bible, the Judeo-Christian-Moslem tradition and science (big bang cosmology) are all in agreement that the universe had a beginning. The second possibility can be discarded on the basis of irrationality. It is irrational to believe that something can create itself out of nothing. In addition, neither science nor the Bible supports this possibility. One or two scientists have suggested this idea, but have been ridiculed even by their professional colleagues. Therefore, we are left with the third possibility, which is the only logical and rational explanation for the origin of the universe.

Science and Religion

Since the question, What is the origin of the universe? lies at the interface of both science and religion, the author believes that we can get closer to the truth if we combine the unequivocal testimony of the Bible with the irrefutable facts of the hard sciences. In this book the author has endeavored to accomplish this without compromising the testimony of the Bible or the evidences of science.

The following are a few examples of the irrefutable facts of science that support the concept of an expanding universe, a concept that is an important part of big bang cosmology:

1. Newton's Law of Universal Gravitation requires the existence of an expanding or a contracting universe.
2. Einstein's general theory of relativity is consistent with an expanding universe.
3. The "red shift" of receding galaxies (The Doppler Principle) is evidence of an expanding universe.
4. Hubble's Law confirms the existence of an expanding universe.

The unequivocal testimony of the Bible, as stated in the following texts, also supports the idea of an expanding universe:

He hath made the earth by his power, he hath established the world by his wisdom, and hath stretched out the heavens by his discretion.
—Jer. 10:12

He hath made the earth by his power, he hath established the world by his wisdom, and hath stretched out the heavens by his understanding.
—Jer. 51:15

Thus saith God the Lord, he that created the heavens, and stretched them out....

—Isa. 42:5

I have made the earth, and created man upon it: I, *even* my hands, have stretched out the heavens, and all their hosts have I commanded.

—Isa. 45:12

Mine hand also hath laid the foundation of the earth, and my right hand hath spread the heavens: when I call unto them they stand up together.

—Isa. 48:13

It is He that sitteth on the circle of the earth...that stretcheth out the heavens as a curtain, and spreadeth them out as a tent to dwell in.

—Isa. 40:22

Who coverest thyself with light as with a garment: who stretchest out the heavens like a curtain.

—Ps.104:2

Which alone spreadeth out the heavens...

—Job 9:8

    This idea of combining the truths of science and the Bible comes to us from St. Augustine, the greatest apologist of the Christian faith since the apostle Paul, and Albert Einstein, the greatest intellect of the twentieth century. About two thousand years ago, Tertullian, the great church father, asked the question, "What, indeed, has Athens to do with Jerusalem? What concord is there between the [Platonic] Academy and the Church?" Tertullian was really asking, "What has science to do with religion?" In his response, Augustine compared Greek philosophy and science "to the treasures which the Israelites appropriated when they departed from Egypt."[1] Einstein's famous response to Tertullian was, "Science without religion is lame; religion without science is blind."[2] Andrade is on target when he states, "Science has proof but no certainty: religion has certainty but no proof."[3] Perhaps by combining science and religion, we may be able to achieve both certainty and proof in our search for the truth.

In support of this idea of combining the best of the hard sciences with the best of revelation, the noted Bible commentator E.G. White states the following: "God is the author of science.... Rightly understood, science and the written word agree, and each sheds light on the other. Together they lead us to God, by teaching us something of the wise and beneficent laws through which He works."[4]

The primary purpose of this book is to present a coherent model of the origin of the universe based on the revelations of scripture and the facts of the hard sciences.

A Word of Caution

Before we begin a discussion of such a profound and mysterious subject as the origin of the universe, a word of caution is in order. This is a subject that should be approached with the humility of a learner seeking truth. Both the Bible and science provide us with incomplete and sometimes inexplicable databases. Revelation (the Bible) at times is silent, and reason (science) is often bewildered. The Bible (Deut. 29:29) reminds us that "The secret *things belong* unto the Lord our God: but those *things which are* revealed *belong* unto us and to our children for ever...." Also the Heisenberg's Uncertainty Principle in science limits our ability ever to have complete knowledge of physical reality in the domain of the microcosm. This Uncertainty Principle states that it is forever impossible to determine with exactness both the position and the velocity of an electron at the same time. It is with these limitations in mind that this book is written.

References for Preface
1. Mortimer J. Adler, *Great Ideas From the Great Books*, New York: Washington Square Press, Inc., 1963, p. 18.
2. *Science, Philosophy, and Religion: a Symposium-* 1941, ch. 13.
3. John Read, "Science, Literature, and Human Thought," *Journal of Chemical Education.* (March 1960), p. 116.
4. Ellen G. White, *Counsels To Parents, Teachers, and Students Regarding Christian Education*, Mountain View: Pacific Press Publishing Association, 1913, p. 426.

Acknowledgments

The author is very much indebted to the following individuals for their critical reading of the manuscript and their valuable suggestions: Dr. Theo Agard, Dr. Ashton F. E. Gibbons, Dr. Lela M. Gooding, Dr. Justin C. Hamer, Dr. Kenneth LaiHing, Dr. Roy E. Malcolm, Dr. Garland J. Millet, Dr. Londa L. Schmidt, Dr. Rothacker C. Smith, Dr. David Richardson, Dr. Mervyn A. Warren and Dr. James White.

The author is also thankful to Mrs. Shirley B. Bailey, Mrs. Marjorie S. Cooper, Mrs. Shirley C. Iheanacho and Mrs. Edrene G. Malcolm for proofreading the manuscript. In addition, grateful appreciation is expressed to the following individuals who have assisted in the preparation of the manuscript: Star Armstrong, Mrs. Eleanor Eakins, Raquel L. Everett, Gwenné P. Gibbons, Mrs. Flore Hamilton, Shaunda E. Kelly, Charene J. Malcolm, Peter E. Malcolm, Candace M. McGoodwin, and Tiffany M. Williams.

Quotations

In the beginning God created the heaven and the earth.

—Genesis 1:1

This most beautiful system of sun, planets, and comets could only proceed from the counsel and dominion of an intelligent and powerful Being. This Being governs all things, not as the soul of the world, but as Lord over all; and on account of His dominion, He is wont to be called Lord God.

—Sir Isaac Newton

The big bang theory requires a recent origin of the universe that openly invites the concept of creation.

—Fred Hoyle, British Mathematician and Cosmologist

If we accept the big bang theory, and most cosmologists now do, then a "creation" of some sort is forced upon us.

—Barry Parker, Cosmologist

There is no doubt that a parallel exists between the big bang as an event and the Christian notion of creating from nothing.

—George Smoot, Cosmologist

For the scientist who has lived by his faith in the power of reason, the story ends like a bad dream. He has scaled the mountains of ignorance; he is about to conquer the highest peak; as he pulls himself over the final rock, *he is greeted by a band of theologians who have been sitting there for centuries* [emphasis added].

—Robert Jastrow, NASA Cosmologist

CHAPTER 1

The God of Science and the Bible

Faith and the Existence of God

The Importance of Faith

I s there a God who is the Creator? Any serious discussion of biblical cosmology (see chapter 4) must begin by making a logical and rational case for the existence of God. The Bible clearly teaches that no one can prove the existence of God. Moses, the putative author of the book of Job, states the following: "Can you find out the deep things of God, *or* can you by searching find out the limit of the Almighty [explore His depths, ascend to His heights, extend to His breadths and comprehend His infinite] perfection?" (Job 11:7 amplified version).

All attempts to prove (or disprove) the existence of God have been unsuccessful. The reason these attempts have failed is that God in His wisdom and for His own unrevealed purpose has ordained that man should exercise a measure of faith in order to come to know Him. This position is supported by St. Paul, who wrote two thousand years ago, "But without faith it is impossible to please him: for he that cometh to God must believe that he is, and that he is a rewarder of them that diligently seek him" (Heb. 11:6).

Even though God expects us to make the leap of faith in order to know Him, He graciously provides us with generous and ample evidences upon which to base our faith. In support of this, the apostle Paul in his letter to the Romans wrote, "For the invisible things of him from the creation of the world are clearly seen, being understood by the things that are made, even his eternal power and Godhead; so that they are without excuse" (Rom. 1:20).

Seven Arguments for the Existence of God

In philosophy there are several major arguments for the existence of God. Following are some of these arguments.

The Moral or Anthropological Argument. This argument is based on the fact that man has a moral nature, which is manifested by a conscience, a sense of compassion, and an innate desire to attain the highest good (*summum bonum*), even though he does not always succeed. It is argued that the original source of this nature and of this desire in man must be a supreme being since it cannot be his environment.

The Bible supports this thesis: "That was the true Light, which lighteth every man that cometh into the world" (John 1:9). Hans Kung, the dissident Roman Catholic theologian and author of the book, *Does God Exist?* contends that "conscience doth make Christians—or at least theists—of us all."[1]

The Mental Argument. In this argument an omniscient being is offered as the only source for man's ability to reason and perceive himself in the act of thinking. According to C.S. Lewis, the twentieth century's greatest apologist for the Christian faith, "If any thought is valid, an eternal, self-existent reason must exist and must be the source of my own imperfect and intermittent rationality."[2]

The Experiential Argument. This argument is based on the ubiquitous existence of the religious experience—of man's predisposition to worship a being greater than himself.

The Teleological Argument. In this argument an infinitely complex and well-ordered universe is presented as evidence for the existence of an intelligent designer. In 1802, William Paley, an English Archdeacon, reasoned that "...anyone who sees a watch is forced to assume the existence of a watchmaker who made it. The marvels of nature's design, from snowflakes to developing embryos, are comforting buttresses to faith for many people."[3]

The Ontological Argument (a priori). This argument was first proposed by Anselm, the eleventh century Archbishop of Canterbury. It states that since man can conceive of a supreme being who is omnipotent, omniscient and omni-present, and who is "...merciful and gracious, longsuffering, and abundant in goodness and truth..." (Exod. 34:6), such a being must exist. This concept of such a supreme being must originate from a source outside of man himself and argues for the existence of such a supreme being.

The Cosmological or Causal Argument. This argument is also known as *a posteriori* argument. According to Saint Thomas Aquinas, each effect must have a cause, and therefore a continuous chain of causes and effects must extend back into an original cause. Jemison states this argument as follows: "Reason teaches that every effect must have a cause. The universe, this world, intelligent men, exist; they are effects. For them there must be a cause. The original cause must be a supreme, intelligent being."[4]

Dr. Mortimer Adler, of the Great Books fame and the author of the book, *How to Think About God*, makes the following incisive comment:

> Philosophers, such as Hume and Kant, who reject both the ontological and the causal arguments for the existence of God, tend to be agnostics rather than atheists. While denying that we can know God's existence by the evidence of reason or experience, they do not deny that God exists. Our belief in God comes not from reason or experience, but from other sources. For Hume, the source is "faith and divine revelation." For Kant, God's existence is a matter of rational faith, a postulate of the practical reason. "It is morally necessary," he says, "to assume the existence of God."[5]

The Argument from Congruence. This argument states that the belief in a personal God is consistent with our knowledge of who we are and the world in which we live. No other belief provides us with a more satisfying understanding of ourselves and the cosmos.

The Pauline Argument

In addition to the seven arguments presented above, it is interesting to note that the apostle Paul presents an even more powerful argument in his sermon on Mars' Hill. His argument may be called the Pauline or life source argument because it is based on God being the source of life. The apostle Paul told the Athenians: "God that made the world and all things therein, seeing that he is Lord of heaven and earth, dwelleth not in temples made with hands; Neither is worshipped with men's hands, as though he needed any thing, seeing he giveth to all life, and breath, and all things" (Acts 17:24–25). Just as the existence of a complex, well-ordered universe suggests the existence of a designer, likewise the existence of living creatures (life), implies the existence of a life-giver. Even though evolutionists believe in the concept of spontaneous generation (the spontaneous generation or occurrence of life), this has never been observed. No one has ever observed in the physical universe the change from inanimate to animate. On the contrary, the opposite process, from life to death, is ubiquitously pervasive.

Testimonies of Some Great Thinkers

Plato, Greek Philosopher (428–347)

"The world is God's epistle to mankind. His thoughts are flashing upon us from every direction."

"The earth, the sun and stars, and the universe itself, the charming variety of the seasons, demonstrate the existence of a Divinity."

Cicero, Roman Orator (106–43)

"Nature herself has imprinted on the minds of all the idea of God."

Augustine, Church Father, Bishop of Hippo (354–430)

"I believe in order that I might understand."

"Thou hast made us for Thyself and our hearts are restless until they find their rest in Thee."

Nicholas Copernicus, Polish Astronomer (1473–1543)

"In many ways, and with innumerable instruments and gifts, God has endowed us and enabled us to study and know nature. We will advance to the point He has desired us to advance, and we will not attempt to transgress the limits imposed by Him."

Martin Luther, German Theologian (1483–1546)

"God writes the gospel not in the Bible alone, but in the trees and flowers...clouds and stars."

Francis Bacon, British Philosopher (1561–1626)

"There are two books laid before us to study, to prevent our falling into error. First, the volume of the Scriptures, which reveal the will of God; then the volume of the creation, which expresses His power."

Sir Isaac Newton, British Philosopher and Mathematician (1642–1727)

"The most elegant system of suns, planets and comets could only arise from the purpose and sovereignty of an intelligent and mighty being.... He rules them all, not as a soul of the world, but a sovereign Lord of all things."

William Cowper, British Poet (1731–1800)

"Nature is a name for an effect, whose cause is God."

Thomas Paine, British Author (1737–1809)

"The creation is in the Bible of the Deist. He reads in the handwriting of the Creator Himself, the certainty of His existence, and the immutability of His power."

Lord Kelvin, British Physicist and Mathematician (1824–1907)

"If you think strongly enough, you will be forced by science to a belief in God. We must pause, face to face, with the mystery and miracle of creation."

Arthur Compton, American Physicist (1892–1962)

"The chance that a world such as ours should occur without intelligent design becomes more and more remote as we learn of its wonders."

Edward Milne, British Astronomer (1896–1950)

"As to the first cause of the universe…our picture is incomplete without Him [God]…"

Wernher Von Braun, German/American Rocket Engineer (1912–1977)

"Manned space flight is an amazing achievement, but it has opened for mankind thus far only a tiny door for viewing the awesome reaches of space. An outlook through this peephole at the vast mysteries of the universe should only confirm our belief in the certainty of its Creator. I find it as difficult to understand a scientist who does not acknowledge the presence of a superior rationality behind the existence of the universe as it is to comprehend a theologian who would deny the advances of science."

Newton and Einstein On The Existence of God

In applying the scientific method to the biblical view of creation, one observes convincing evidence about the nature of the universe (data) which leads to the view (law) that the universe is a well-ordered and intricately designed system that must have been created by a supreme intelligence. It may be argued that Sir Isaac Newton, the discoverer of the Law of Universal Gravitation and the inventor of Calculus, was using the scientific method when he reasoned as follows:

This universe exists, and by that one impossible fact declares itself a miracle; postulates an infinite Power within itself, a whole greater than any part: a unity sustaining all, binding all worlds into one. This is the mystery, the unquestioned miracle that we know, implying every attribute of God.[6]

It is rather interesting to note that Sir Isaac Newton reasoned from the existence of a magnificently ordered and mysterious universe to the existence of God. Albert Einstein, using Newton's line of reasoning, also arrived at the conclusion that there exists a "superior reasoning power," which he called God. Listen to his comments:

The most beautiful and most profound emotion we can experience is the sensation of the mystical. It is the sower of all true sciences. He to whom this emotion is a stranger, who can no longer wonder and stand rapt in awe, is as good as dead. To know that what is impenetrable to us really exists, manifesting itself as the highest wisdom and the most radiant beauty which our dull faculties can comprehend only in their most primitive forms—this knowledge, this feeling is at the center of true religiousness.[7]

The cosmic religious experience is the strongest and noblest mainspring of scientific research.[8] My religion [he says] consists of a humble admiration of the illimitable superior spirit who reveals himself in the slight details we are able to perceive with our frail and feeble minds. That deeply emotional conviction of the presence of a superior reasoning power, which is revealed in the incomprehensible universe, forms my idea of God.[9]

In summary, we find Sir Isaac Newton and Albert Einstein, two of the most intellectually gifted and brilliant men that ever lived, to whom we owe most of our understanding of the universe, reasoning from the existence of the universe to the existence of God.

The Credibility of the Bible

The Bible Is the Word of God

The belief that the Bible is the word of God is based on the incredible uniqueness of the Bible, its "more sure word of prophecy," its revelation of scientific truths centuries before they were discovered, and the testimonies of its writers. Note the testimonies of the following Bible writers:

Moses. "So Moses went down unto the people, and spake unto them. And God spake all these words, saying..." (Exod. 19:25–20:1). "And Moses called all Israel, and said unto them, Hear, O Israel, the statutes and judgments which I speak in your ears this day, that ye may learn them, and keep, and do them" (Deut. 5:1).

The prophet Isaiah. "Hear the word of the Lord, ye rulers of Sodom; give ear unto the law of our God, ye people of Gomorrah (Isa. 1:10).

The prophet Jeremiah. "Moreover the word of the Lord came unto me saying..." (Jer. 1:11). "And the word of the Lord came unto me the second time, saying..." (Jer. 1:13).

The prophet Ezekiel. "The word of the Lord came expressly unto Ezekiel the priest..." (Ezek. 1:3).

The prophet Hosea. "The word of the Lord that came unto Hosea..." (Hos. 1:1).

The prophet Joel. "The word of the Lord that came to Joel..." (Joel 1:1).

The prophet Amos. "Thus saith the Lord..." (Amos 1:3).

The prophet Jonah. "Now the word of the Lord came unto Jonah..." (Jon. 1:1)

The prophet Micah. "The word of the Lord that came to Micah..." (Mic. 1:1).

The prophet Zephaniah. "The word of the Lord which came unto Zephaniah..." (Zeph. 1:1).

The prophet Haggai. "In the second year of Darius the king, in the sixth month, in the first day of the month, came the word of the Lord by Haggai the prophet..." (Hag. 1:1).

The prophet Zechariah. "In the eighth month, in the second year of Darius, came the word of the Lord unto Zechariah..." (Zech. 1:1).

The prophet Malachi. "The burden of the word of the Lord to Israel by Malachi" (Mal. 1:1).

The apostle Paul. "For this cause also thank we God without ceasing, because, when ye received the word of God which ye heard of us, ye received *it* not *as* the word of men, but as it is in truth, the word of God, which effectually worketh also in you that believe" (1 Thes. 2:13).

The apostle Peter. "But the word of the Lord endureth for ever. And this is the word which by the gospel is preached unto you" (1 Pet. 1:25).

Jesus Christ. "The revelation of Jesus Christ, which God gave unto him, to shew unto his servants things which must shortly come to pass; and he sent and signified *it* by his angel unto his servant John: Who bare record of the word of God, and of the testimony of Jesus Christ, and of all things that he saw" (Rev. 1:1–2).

It has been estimated that there are approximately 1,500 statements in the Bible supporting the statement that the Bible is the word of God.

The Uniqueness of the Bible

There is no other book that has ever been written that is comparable to the Bible in uniqueness. It is essentially a library of sixty-six books, written in three languages by forty authors having different professional and vocational backgrounds, over a period of 1,500 years. In spite of its number of different authors and the long span of time over which it was written, the Bible has a consistency and a coherency that is incredible.

Prophecy—the Predictive Factor

The principal difference between the hard sciences like biology, chemistry and physics and the soft sciences like economics, psychology and sociology is the predictive ability that characterizes the hard sciences. In his book, *A Brief History of Time*, Stephen Hawking, the British mathematical physicist, considered by some to be the successor of Albert Einstein, has articulated the modern goal of science as follows, "In effect, we have redefined the task of science to be the discovery of laws that would enable us to predict events up to the limits set by the uncertainty principle."[10]

It is interesting to note that when God speaks to mankind about His unique existence, He cites, one, His ability to create and, two, His ability to foretell the future. Note Isaiah 40:25–26: "To whom then will ye liken me, or shall I be equal? saith the Holy One. Lift up your eyes on high, and behold who hath created these things...." And also in Isaiah 46:9–10 He says: "Remember the former things of old: for I am God, and there is none else; I am God, and there is none like me, declaring the end from the beginning, and from ancient times the things that are not yet done...."

A consideration of some of the amazingly accurately fulfilled prophecies in the Bible, especially those pertaining to ancient Israel, should compel us to accept the reliability, authenticity and credibility of the Bible and to consider what it has to say to us about God, about the origin of the universe and about man's existence in the cosmos.

Declaring the reliability and the origin of the Holy Scriptures, the apostle Peter wrote, "We have also a more sure word of prophecy; whereunto ye do well that ye take heed, as unto a light that shineth in a dark place, until the day dawn, and the day star arise in your hearts: Knowing this first, that no prophecy of the scripture is of any private interpretation. For the prophecy came not in old time by the will of man: but holy men of God spake as they were moved by the Holy Ghost" (2 Pet. 1:19–21).

It is interesting to note that the apostle Peter stated that "we have also a more sure word of prophecy" after telling us about his eyewitness account of the transfiguration of Jesus Christ. Listen to his words: "For we have not followed cunningly devised fables, when we made known unto you the power and coming of our Lord Jesus Christ, but were eyewitnesses of his majesty" (2 Pet. 1:16). In brief, the apostle Peter is telling us that the "more sure word of prophecy" is even more compelling as evidence than his eyewitness account of the transfiguration. In support of the apostle Peter's declaration, the apostle Paul wrote that "All scripture is given by inspiration of God, and is profitable for doctrine, for reproof, for correction, for instruction in righteousness" (2 Tim. 3:16).

Today scientists have great faith in the validity of Einstein's theory of relativity. This faith is based on the fact that so many predictions of this theory have been experimentally verified. Let us consider the following examples:

1. Einstein's theory predicted that because of the gravitational field of the sun, the light from distant stars should bend when passing close to the sun.

2. His theory also predicted that no object or particle having mass can travel faster than the speed of light and that the speed of light is a constant. This prediction is based on his famous equation $E = mc^2$, in which E is the energy, m is the mass, and c is the velocity of light. Rearranging this equation to the following form $E/m = c^2$, we see that if c is constant, E/m must also be constant. Therefore, if E (energy) increases, m (mass) must also increase proportionately. It has been found that when an electron is energized to have a velocity that is 90 percent of the speed of light, its mass doubles. The tremendous amount of energy released when matter is converted into energy (nuclear reactors and the atomic bomb) also confirms Einstein's equation.

3. Einstein's assertion that the speed of light is a constant is in harmony with the results of the Michelson-Morley experiment of 1881.

Just as the element of predictability gives credibility to the theory of relativity, likewise it is found that the element of predictability (fulfilled prophecies) gives credibility to the Bible, which is the Word of God. These fulfilled prophecies are as much a reality as the fulfilled predictions based on the equation $E=mc^2$.

From the above it is evident that the ability to predict future events is an intrinsic characteristic of both the hard sciences and the Bible. Science predicts future events through its laws and *successful* theories. The Bible predicts the future through the foreknowledge of an omniscient God.

The Bible prophecies and their fulfillments which will be discussed below were chosen because they are straightforward and do not require any interpretation. In each case the fulfillment is clear and unambiguous.

Non-Messianic Prophecies

There are a number of prophecies concerning ancient Israel that have been fulfilled with remarkable accuracy. These fulfilled prophecies speak eloquently and convincingly about the credibility of the Bible to everyone with an open mind.

The four-hundred-year prophecy. In this remarkable prophecy, God predicted that the children of Israel (the descendants of Abraham, Isaac and Jacob) would be slaves in Egypt approximately four hundred years. *Prophecy:* Speaking to Abraham, God said, "Know of a surety that thy seed shall be a stranger in a land that is not theirs, and shall serve them; and they shall afflict them four hundred years" (Gen. 15:13).

The accurate fulfillment of this prophecy is recorded in Exodus 12:40–41. *Fulfillment:* "Now the sojourning of the children of Israel, who dwelt in Egypt, was four hundred and thirty years. And it came to pass at the end of the four hundred and thirty years, even the selfsame day it came to pass, that all the hosts of the Lord went out from the land of Egypt" (Exod.12:40–41). *Note:* the discrepancy between the four hundred years mentioned in Genesis 15:13 and the 430 years mentioned in Exodus 12:40–41 is explained by some theologians by noting that the affliction of the children of Israel did not actually begin until sometime after the death of Joseph (probably thirty years) when "there arose a new king over Egypt, which knew not Joseph" (Exod. 1:8).

The seventy-year prophecy. Prior to the Babylonian captivity of the children of Israel, God predicted through His prophet Jeremiah that the children of Israel would be held captive in Babylon for seventy years, and then would be permitted to return to the homeland. *Prophecy:* The prophet Jeremiah wrote, "And this whole land shall be a desolation, and an astonishment; and these nations shall serve the king of Babylon seventy years. And it shall come to pass, when seventy years are accomplished, that I will punish the king of Babylon…" (Jer. 25:11–12). "For thus saith the Lord, That after seventy years be accomplished at Babylon I will visit you, and perform my good word toward you, in causing you to return to this place" (Jer.29:10).

Fulfillment: The prophet Daniel indicated his knowledge of the prophecy when he wrote, "In the first year of his reign I Daniel understood by books the number of the years, whereof the word of the Lord came to Jeremiah the prophet, that he would accomplish seventy years in the desolations of Jerusalem" (Dan. 9:2). The remarkable fulfillment of this prophecy is recorded by the scribe and prophet Ezra:

> Now in the first year of Cyrus king of Persia, that the word of the Lord by the mouth of Jeremiah might be fulfilled, the Lord stirred up the spirit of Cyrus king of Persia, that he made a proclamation throughout all his kingdom, and put it also in writing, saying, Thus saith Cyrus king of Persia, The Lord God of heaven hath given me all the kingdoms of the earth; and he hath charged me to build him a house at Jerusalem, which is in Judah.
> Who is there among you of all his people? his God be with him, and let him go up to Jerusalem, which is in Judah....
>
> —Ezra 1:1–3

Prophecy concerning Cyrus, the great king. Another truly remarkable prophecy that is related to the seventy-year prophecy described above is the prophecy concerning Cyrus, king of Persia. Approximately *150 years before the reign of this king*, God predicted his birth, and his name. He also predicted that Cyrus would authorize the emancipation of the children of Israel, the rebuilding of Jerusalem and the restoration of the temple at the end of the Babylonian captivity. *Prophecy:* Recording this prophecy, the prophet Isaiah wrote:

> That saith of Cyrus, He is my shepherd, and shall perform all my pleasure: even saying to Jerusalem, Thou shalt be built; and to the temple, Thy foundation shall be laid.
>
> —Isa. 44:28

> Thus saith the Lord to his anointed, to Cyrus, whose right hand I have holden, to subdue nations before him; and I will loose the loins of kings, to open before him the two leaved gates; and the gates shall not be shut;" "For Jacob my servant's sake, and Israel mine elect, I have even called thee by thy name: I have surnamed thee, though thou hast not known me. I am the Lord, and there is none else, there is no God besides me.... I have raised him up in righteousness, and I will direct all his ways: he shall build my city, and he shall let go my captives, not for price nor reward, saith the Lord of hosts.
>
> —Isa. 45:1, 4, 5, 13

For thus saith the LORD, That after seventy years be accomplished at Babylon I will visit you, and perform my good word toward you, in causing you to return to this place.

—(Jer. 29:10)

Fulfillment: With remarkable accuracy this prophecy was fulfilled at the end of the Babylonian captivity. In describing the fulfillment of this prophecy, the prophet Ezra wrote:

Now in the first year of Cyrus King of Persia, that the word of the Lord by the mouth of Jeremiah might be fulfilled, the Lord stirred up the spirit of Cyrus king of Persia, that he made a proclamation throughout all his kingdom, and put it also in writing, saying, Thus saith Cyrus king of Persia, The Lord God of heaven hath given me all the kingdoms of the earth; and he hath charged me to build him a house at Jerusalem, which is in Judah. (Ezra 1:1–2) But in the first year of Cyrus the king of Babylon the same king Cyrus made a decree to build this house of God.

—Ezra 5:13

The destruction of Jerusalem foretold. One of several important prophecies given by Christ during the final weeks of His ministry was the prophecy pertaining to the destruction of Jerusalem. With remarkable accuracy and exactness, Christ predicted the details of this tremendous tragedy for the Jewish nation. He described the following: one, the nature of the siege, two, the extent of the destruction, and, three, the terrible effects upon the inhabitants of the city. In addition, He told His followers to flee to the mountains for safety. Three historians record his prophecy in their writings:

And Jesus went out, and departed from the temple: and his disciples came to him for to shew him the buildings of the temple…. And Jesus said unto them, See ye not all these things? Verily I say unto you, There shall not be left here one stone upon another, that shall not be thrown down.

—Matt. 24:1–2

And as he went out of the temple, one of his disciples saith unto him, Master, see what manner of stones and what buildings are here! And Jesus answering said unto him, Seest thou these great buildings? There shall not be left one stone upon another, that shall not be thrown down.

—Mark 13:1–2

Prophecy: And when ye shall see Jerusalem compassed with armies, then know that the desolation thereof is nigh. Then let them which are in Judea flee to the mountains; and let them which are in the midst of it depart out; and let not them that are in the countries enter thereinto.

—Luke 21:20–21

And when he was come near, he beheld the city, and wept over it, Saying, If thou hadst known, even thou, at least in this thy day, the things which belong unto thy peace! But now they are hid from thine eyes. For the days shall come upon thee, and thine enemies shall cast a trench about thee, and compass thee round, and keep thee in on every side, and shall lay thee even with the ground, and thy children within thee; and they shall not leave in thee one stone upon another; because thou knewest not the time of thy visitation.

—Luke 19:41–44

O Jerusalem, Jerusalem, *thou* that killest the prophets, and stonest them which are sent unto thee, how often would I have gathered thy children together, even as a hen gathereth her chicken under *her* wings, and ye would not! Behold, your house is left unto you desolate.

—Matt. 23:37–38

Fulfillment: Describing the fulfillment of this prophecy, the noted Bible commentator E.G. White writes:

Not one Christian perished in the destruction of Jerusalem. Christ had given His disciples warning, and all who believed His words watched for the promised sign.[11]

After the Romans under Cestius had surrounded the city, they unexpectedly abandoned the siege when everything seemed favorable for an immediate attack. The besieged, despairing of successful resistance, were on the point of surrender, when the Roman general withdrew his forces without the least apparent reason. But God's merciful providence was directing events for the good of His own people. The promised sign had been given to the waiting Christians, and now an opportunity was offered for all who would, to obey the Saviour's warning. Events were so overruled that neither Jews nor Romans should hinder the flight of the Christians. Upon the retreat of Cestius, the Jews, sallying from Jerusalem, pursued after his retiring army; and while both forces were thus fully engaged, the Christians had an opportunity to leave the city.... Without delay they fled to a place of safety—the city of Pella, in the land of Perea, beyond Jordan.[12]

Terrible were the calamities that fell upon Jerusalem when the siege was resumed by Titus.[13]

In describing how Titus endeavored to save the temple and how he was overruled by divine fiat, E.G. White declares:

Like one entranced, he looked from the crest of Olivet upon the magnificent temple and gave command that not one stone of it be touched.[14]

In vain were the efforts of Titus to save the temple; One greater than he had declared that not one stone was to be left upon another.[15]

Josephus himself, in a most eloquent appeal, entreated them to surrender, to save themselves, their city, and their place of worship. But his words were answered with bitter curses. Darts were hurled at him, their last human mediator, as he stood pleading with them.[16]

Both the city and the temple were razed to their foundations, and the ground upon which the holy house had stood was "plowed like a field" (Jer. 26:18). In the siege and the slaughter that followed, more than a million of the people perished....[17]

A most interesting statement concerning the destruction of Jerusalem is made by Florence Armstrong Grondal in her book, *The Romance of Astronomy*, "Josephus tells us that the destruction of Jerusalem in AD 69 was caused by no less than the sword-shaped comet which pierced the heavens above the city!"[19]

The destruction of Tyre. The prophecy concerning the destruction of Tyre, with its accurate fulfillment, is one that provides convincing evidence of the credibility of the Bible. Centuries ago God predicted through His prophet Ezekiel that Tyre would be destroyed and never be rebuilt. With amazing accuracy, God also predicted that its fertile soil would be removed, leaving a barren landscape and rocks for fishermen to dry their nets.

Prophecy:

Therefore thus saith the Lord God; Behold, I am against thee, O Tyrus, and will cause many nations to come up against thee, as the sea causeth his waves to come up. And they shall destroy the walls of Tyrus, and break down her towers: I will also scrape her dust from her, and make her like the top of a rock. It shall be a place for the spreading of nets in the midst of the sea: for I have spoken it, saith the Lord God: and it shall become a spoil to the nations.

—Ezek. 26:3–5

And I will make thee like the top of a rock: thou shalt be a place to spread nets upon; thou shalt be built no more: for I the Lord have spoken it, saith the Lord God.

—Ezek. 26:14

Fulfillment: In the year 322 BC, the armies of Alexander the Great (consisting of many nations) did what no other armies had previously been able to do. Alexander the Great not only conquered that part of Tyre that was located on the mainland but he built a causeway from the mainland to the island portion of Tyre. This enabled his army to demolish the previously impregnable defenses of Tyre. Then as God's instrument of destruction, he did exactly what God had predicted he would do centuries before. Alexander the Great ordered his army to scrape the fertile soil from the island city of Tyre. Today, Tyre still remains unbuilt as God had predicted and still remains a barren and rocky landscape for fishermen to dry their nets and for skeptics to ponder.

The Diaspora. Here is a prophecy and its fulfillment that are still evident today and should convince the most enduring skeptic that the Bible is indeed credible. Speaking through Moses, God warned Israel that if they did not hearken unto Him, He would scatter them among the nations of the earth:

Prophecy:

But it shall come to pass, if thou wilt not hearken unto the voice of the Lord thy God, to observe to do all his commandments and his statutes which I command thee this day; that all these curses shall come upon thee, and overtake thee.

—Deut. 28:15

And the Lord shall scatter thee among all people, from the one end of the earth even unto the other; and there thou shalt serve other gods, which neither thou nor thy fathers have known, even wood and stone.

—Deut. 28:64

Fulfillment: History tells us that between 734 BC and AD 70 there were several deportations of Jews from their homeland. Deportations occurred under the Assyrians, the Babylonians, and the Romans. From AD 70 until 1948, no independent Jewish state existed. Today large populations and communities of Jews are still found in the former Soviet Union, in Eastern and Western Europe, in the United States, and in many other countries.

Science Supports the Scriptures

One of the most convincing arguments in support of the credibility of the Bible is the fact that the Bible speaks about certain scientific phenomena centuries before their discoveries by scientists. This is a fact that is often overlooked by those who question the credibility of the Bible. In support of this thesis, the great British astronomer, Sir J.F. William Herschel (1792–1871), the discoverer of the planet Uranus, stated emphatically, "All human discoveries seem to be made only for the purpose of confirming more strongly the truths that come from on high and are contained in the Bible."[18]

Here are some examples of how the Bible has revealed scientific truths centuries before they were discovered by modern science:

The Breath of Life

"And the Lord God formed man of the dust of the ground, and breathed into his nostrils the breath of life; and man became a living soul."
—Gen. 2:7

"Thou hidest thy face, they are troubled: thou takest away their breath, they die, and return to their dust."
—Ps. 104:29

Centuries before the development of modern biochemistry, the Bible revealed the absolute necessity of respiration (the breath of life) for human life. It revealed that Adam did not become a living creature until respiration began. Even though cellular respiration begins at the time of conception, the full respiratory system does not begin to function until birth. Therefore, it is correct to say that just as life outside the womb begins at birth and ends at death, respiration outside the womb likewise begins at birth and ends at death.

Modern biochemistry tells us that any substance capable of preventing respiration from occurring is toxic and can become lethal. For example, carbon monoxide, a deadly gas, can combine with hemoglobin (the oxygen carrier of blood) to form a very stable compound. The formation of this compound reduces the availability of oxygen to the cells and leads to death. Likewise, hydrogen cyanide, a deadly gas used in gas chambers to implement capital punishment, causes death by shutting down the electron transport system which is an absolute necessity for cellular respiration.

The Innumerable Stars

> "As the host of heaven cannot be numbered, neither the sand of the sea measured: so will I multiply the seed of David my servant, and the Levites that minister unto me."
>
> —Jer. 33:22

Someone has said that during the time of Jeremiah, astronomers estimated that there were only about five thousand stars in the heavens. But the prophet Jeremiah was inspired to proclaim that the host (stars) of heaven cannot be numbered. Today, modern astronomy tells us that there are approximately one hundred billion (1.0×10^{11}) stars in our galaxy (the Milky Way) and that there are approximately one hundred billion galaxies similar to ours. From this, we conclude that the estimated number of stars in the universe is on the order of 1.0×10^{22} or ten thousand billion, billion, but we have to admit that, as Jeremiah asserted, we do not have the ability to make an absolute reckoning.

Pleiades, Orion, and Arcturus

The Book of Job is a classic example of how the Bible revealed scientific truths centuries before they were discovered by modern science. Written by the prophet Moses, who was also the author of the first five books of the Bible, the Book of Job is one of the earliest books ever written. Moses records a conversation between God and Job in which God asks Job if he, Job, could do that which God was constantly doing: "Canst thou bind the sweet influences of Pleiades, or loose the bands of Orion? Canst thou bring forth Mazzaroth in his season? Or canst thou guide Arcturus with his sons?" (Job 38:31–32).

The Pleiades is a group of seven stars to the naked eye. However, modern astronomy reveals it to be a cluster of approximately 250 stars when viewed with a telescope. It may be argued that the expression in Job, "bind the sweet influences" suggests the cluster nature of the Pleiades.

Modern astronomy reveals that the band of Orion consists of three stars in the belt of this mighty hunter, which, at this moment in eternity, happens to be in a straight line. But each star is actually moving in a different direction. These stars are like three ships on the ocean that happen to meet temporarily to form a line, but each ship is headed in a different direction. It is most interesting to note that the Bible revealed the loosening of this band centuries before modern astronomy discovered this fact.

Modern astronomy tells us that Arcturus travels so fast that it is considered to be a runaway star. However, the Bible suggested this fact centuries ago with the expression "canst thou guide Arcturus?".

The Expanding Universe

The Bible suggested the expansion of the universe long before its discovery by Edwin Hubble in 1929. The expression "stretched out the heavens" definitely suggests an expanding universe.

> He hath made the earth by his power, he hath established the world by his wisdom, and hath stretched out the heavens by his discretion.
> —Jer. 10:12

> He hath made the earth by his power, he hath established the world by his wisdom, and hath stretched out the heaven by his understanding.
> —Jer. 51:15

> Thus saith God the Lord, he that created the heavens, and stretched them out....
> —Isa. 42:5

> Who coverest *thyself* with light as with a garment: who stretchest out the heavens like a curtain.
> —Ps. 104:2

In 1929 the great American Astronomer, Edwin Hubble, discovered that certain characteristic lines in the spectra of stars in distant galaxies had a red shift. Based on the Doppler Effect this red shift indicated to Hubble that these galaxies were moving away from us. He also discovered that the more distant the galaxies, the faster they were moving away from us. Thus, he had discovered an expanding universe. (Please see Chapter 6 for more details on the expanding universe.)

The Birth and Death of Stars

> "And, Thou, Lord, in the beginning hast laid the foundation of the earth; and the heavens are the works of thine hands: They shall perish; but thou remainest; and they shall wax old as doth a garment."
>
> —Heb. 1:10–11

Here is a remarkable pronouncement in the Bible concerning the transitory existence of the heavens (stars) centuries before science discovered this phenomenon. In this particular text, God the Father is addressing God the Son and is comparing the eternal existence of Christ with the transitory existence of the heavens. In her book, *The Romance of Astronomy*, Florence Armstrong Grondal describes the progression of stars from birth to death:

> Throughout the sky are young stars, adult stars, and stars whose light has almost flickered out, for stars, we find, even as all other things in Nature, have a limited span of life. This life may last for untold ages but as surely as stars are formed, so do they die. …Recent studies have revealed the fact that stars when young are huge and red. This early stage is called the giant stage. Antares, Betelgeuse, Arcturus, and Aldebaran are examples of stars at the beginning of their careers.
>
> …The blue stars are in the prime of life, intensely hot and brilliant, and glow with a temperature of perhaps 10,000 degrees at their luminous surfaces. With a gradual rise and fall of temperature, stars burn, even as earthly flames, through a continuous series of colors— generally speaking, red, yellow, blue, yellow, red—and all of which bear a special meaning to an astronomer. The yellow stars, like our sun, are middle-aged; the dwarf red stars, old, like a dying ember."[19]

Today, it is believed that some very old stars may eventually become white dwarfs, then neutron stars, and finally black holes.

Limitations of Science

In spite of the phenomenal successes of science in harnessing nuclear energy, putting a man on the moon, mapping the human genome, et cetera, science has its limitations. Even at the present time when the volume of scientific knowledge may be doubling every ten years or fewer, scientists can no longer boast as they did fifty years ago: "The difficult things we do right away; the impossible may take a little longer." Science has encountered staggering difficulties both in the microcosmos (the infinitesimally small universe of the atom) and the macrocosmos (the infinitely large universe of receding galaxies). These difficulties have caused even the most optimistic disciples of science to question whether science can ever furnish us with complete knowledge or truth about the nature of physical reality. Indeed the biblical pronouncement, "Ever learning, and never able to come to the knowledge of the truth" (2 Tim. 3:7), may appropriately be applied to science.

Quite apropos is the parable of the German dramatist Lessing Gotthold Ephraim, (1729–1781). In his play, *Nathan, the Wise,* Lessing has a dialogue in which God confronts man and asks him to make a choice, "In my left hand I have the virtue called *eternal search for truth;* in my right hand I have *absolute eternal truth*. I would give you which-ever you wish." To this, man, after some soul-searching, turns to God and said, "Please open your left hand for me. I want that virtue called the *eternal search for truth*. The contents of your right hand would be incomprehensible, they would be stagnating."[20]

The limitations of science are fitly portrayed in the words of Lincoln Barnett:

> Man's inescapable impasse is that he himself is part of the world he seeks to explore; his body and proud brain are mosaics of the same elemental particles that compose the dark, drifting dust clouds of interstellar space; he is, in the final analysis, merely an ephemeral conformation of the primordial space-time field. Standing midway between macrocosm and microcosm he finds barriers on every side and can perhaps but marvel, as St. Paul did nineteen hundred years ago, that "the world was created by the word of God so that what is seen was made out of things which do not appear."[21]

And we can add to this the sobering thought of Sir Arthur Stanley Eddington, English astronomer (1882–1944): "We have found a strange footprint on the shores of the unknown. We have devised profound theories one after another to account for its origin. At last, we have succeeded in reconstructing the creature that made the footprint. And Lo! It is our own."[22]

Summary Statement

In view of all the evidence presented in this chapter, including a total of six amazing, accurately fulfilled prophecies and the ability of the Bible to speak of scientific phenomena centuries before their discovery by modern science, how can anyone still continue to consider the Bible to be a book of myths?

Before closing this chapter, let us consider one additional thought. Long before the existence of such concepts as global pollution and nuclear holocausts, the writer of the Book of Revelation was inspired to write about man's ability to destroy the earth. Notice the following prophetic statement, which was written two thousand years ago and which is now realistically possible: "And the nations were angry, and thy wrath is come, and the time of the dead, that they should be judged, and that thou shouldest give reward unto thy servants the prophets, and to the saints, and them that fear thy name, small and great; and shouldest destroy them which destroy the earth" (Rev. 11:18).

1   *Time*, "Modernizing the Case for God," April 7, 1980, p. 65.
2   Ibid., "Modernizing the Case for God," p. 66.
3   Ibid., "Modernizing the Case for God," p. 66.
4   T.H. Jemison, *Christian Beliefs*, Mountain View: Pacific Press Pub. Association.,1959, p. 72.
5   Mortimer J. Adler, *Great Ideas from The Great Books*, New York: Washington Square Press, Inc., 1963, p. 141.
6   Phillip L. Knox, *Sky Wonders*, Mountain View: Pacific Press Publishing Association, 1945, p. 17.

7 Lincoln Barnett, *The Universe and Dr. Einstein*, New York: William Sloan Associates, 1948, p. 105.

8 Barnett, p. 105.

9 Barnett, p. 106.

10 Stephen Hawking, *A Brief History of Time: From the Big Bang to Black Holes*, New York, Bantam Books, 1990, p. 173.

11 Ellen G. White, *The Great Controversy*, Boise, Idaho: Pacific Press Publishing Association, 1950, p. 30.

12 White, pp. 30-31.

13 White, p. 31.

14 White, p. 32.

15 White, p. 33.

16 White, p. 33.

17 White, p. 35.

18 Phillip L. Knox, *Sky Wonders*, Mountain View: Pacific Press Publishing Association, 1945, pp. 15–16.

19 Florence Armstrong Grondal, *The Romance of Astronomy: The Music of the Spheres*, New York: The Macmillan Company, 1942, p. 236.

20 From a series of lectures on the history and philosophy of Science and Mathematics given at American University during the summer of 1963. {also see *The Oxford Dictionary of Quotations*, 3rd ed. 1979}.

21 Lincoln Barnett, *The Universe and Dr. Einstein*, New York: William Sloane Associates, 1948, p. 114.

22 From a series of lectures on the history and philosophy of Science and Mathematics given at American University during the summer of 1963.

CHAPTER TWO

Fiat Creation and Creation Ex Nihilo

Fiat Creation

Fiat creation literally means "creation by command." The Psalmist David speaks eloquently of the creation of the universe by means of fiat creation: "By the word of the Lord were the heavens made; and all the host of them by the breath of his mouth. For he spake, and it was done; he commanded, and it stood fast" (Ps. 33:6, 9). "Let them praise the name of the LORD: for He commanded, and they were created" (Ps. 148:5).

Creation Ex Nihilo

The Latin expression, *ex nihilo,* literally means out of nothing. Therefore creation ex nihilo means "creation out of nothing." And we are indebted to the apostle Paul for the concept of creation ex nihilo: "Through faith we understand that the worlds were framed by the word of God, so that things which are seen were not made of things which do appear" (Heb. 11:3). Weymouth renders Hebrews 11:3 as follows, "What is seen does not owe its existence to that which is visible." Thus the Bible tells us that the Creator-God was not indebted to pre-existing matter in the creation of the universe.

On this point, the prophet Isaiah is very descriptive. Let us note the similarity in language used by the prophet Isaiah in describing the creation of the heavens and the earth: "Mine hand also hath laid the foundation of the earth, and my right hand hath spanned the heavens: when I call unto them, they stand up together" (Isa. 48:13).

On this point, the noted Bible commentator E.G. White is unequivocal:

> The theory that God did not create matter when He brought the world into existence is without foundation. In the formation of our world, God was not indebted to preexisting matter. On the contrary, all things, material or spiritual, stood up before the Lord Jehovah at His voice and were created for His own purpose. The heavens and all of the host of them, the earth and all the things therein, are not only the work of His hand; they came into existence by the breath of His mouth.[1]

"The Creation"—By James Weldon Johnson

In his classic poem titled, *The Creation*, James Weldon Johnson captures the beautiful folklore language and thinking of early Afro-Americans about the beginning of the universe. Even though the science and the theology expressed in it are imaginative and primitive, the superb poem presents a beautiful picture of omnipotence in action and reverberates with the ideas of fiat creation and creation ex nihilo.

The Creation[2]
By James Weldon Johnson

And God stepped out on space,
And he looked around and said:
I'm lonely—
I'll make me a world.
And far as the eye of God could see
Darkness covered everything,
Blacker than a hundred midnights
Down in a cypress swamp.

Then God smiled,
And the light broke,
And the darkness rolled up on one side,
And the light stood shining on the other,
And God said: That's good!
Then God reached out and took the light in his hands,
And God rolled the light around in his hands
Until he made the sun;
And he set that sun a-blazing in the heavens.
And the light that was left from making the sun
God gathered it up in a shining ball
And flung it against the darkness,
Spangling the night with the moon and stars.
Then down between
The darkness and the light
He hurled the world;
And God said: That's good!
Then God himself stepped down—
And the sun was on his right hand,
And the moon was on his left;
The stars were clustered about his head,
And the earth was under his feet.
And God walked, and where he trod
His footsteps hollowed the valleys out
And bulged the mountains up.
Then he stopped and looked and saw
That the earth was hot and barren.
So God stepped over to the edge of the world
And he spat out the seven seas—
He batted his eyes, and the lightnings flashed—
He clapped his hands, and the thunders rolled—
And the waters above the earth came down,
The cooling waters came down.
Then the green grass sprouted,
And the little red flowers blossomed,
The pine tree pointed his finger to the sky,
And the oak spread out his arms,
The lakes cuddled down in the hollows of the ground,
And the rivers ran down to the sea;

And God smiled again,
And the rainbow appeared,
And curled itself around his shoulder.
Then God raised his arm and he waved his hand
Over the sea and over the land,
And he said: Bring forth! Bring forth!
And quicker than God could drop his hand,
Fishes and fowls
And beasts and birds
Swam the rivers and the seas,
Roamed the forests and the woods,
And split the air with their wings.
And God said: That's good!
Then God walked around,
And God looked around
On all that he had made.
He looked at his sun,
And he looked at his moon,
And he looked at his little stars;
He looked on his world
With all its living things,
And God said: I'm lonely still.
Then God sat down—
On the side of a hill where he could think;
By a deep, wide river he sat down;
With his head in his hands,
God thought and thought,
Till he thought: I'll make me a man!
Up from the bed of the river
God scooped the clay;
And by the bank of the river
He kneeled him down;
And there was the great God Almighty
Who lit the sun and fixed it in the sky,
Who flung the stars to the most far corner of the night,
Who rounded the earth in the middle of his hand;
This great God,
Like a mammy bending over her baby,
Kneeled down in the dust

Toiling over a lump of clay
Till he shaped it in his own image;
Then into it he blew the breath of life,
And man became a living soul.
Amen. Amen.

Testimonies of the Bible Writers

The Testimony of Moses

In the beginning God created the heaven and the earth.

—Gen. 1:1

Remember the Sabbath day, to keep it holy. Six days shalt thou labor, and do all thy work: But the seventh day is the Sabbath of the Lord thy God: in it thou shalt not do any work, thou, nor thy son, nor thy daughter, thy manservant, nor thy maidservant, nor thy cattle, nor thy stranger that is within thy gates: For in six days the Lord made heaven and earth, the sea, and all that in them is, and rested the seventh day: wherefore the Lord blessed the Sabbath day, and hallowed it.

—Ex 20:8-11

Where wast thou when I laid the foundations of the earth? Declare, if thou hast understanding.

—Job 38:4

Lord, thou hast been our dwelling place in all generations. Before the mountains were brought forth, or ever thou hadst formed the earth and the world, even from everlasting to everlasting, thou *art* God.

—Ps. 90:1, 2

The Testimony of Nehemiah

"Thou, *even* thou, *art* Lord alone; thou hast made heaven, the heaven of heavens, with all their host, the earth, and all *things* that *are* therein, the seas, and all that *is* therein, and thou preservest them all; and the host of heaven worshippeth thee."

—Neh. 9:6

Testimony of David

For all the gods of the people are idols: but the Lord made the heavens.

—1 Chron. 16:26

When I consider thy heavens, the work of thy fingers, the moon and the stars, which thou hast ordained; What is man, that thou art mindful of him? And the son of man, that thou visitest him?

—Ps. 8:3,4

The heavens declare the glory of God; and the firmament sheweth His handywork. Day unto day uttereth speech, and night unto night sheweth knowledge. There is no speech nor language, where their voice is not heard. Their line is gone out through all the earth, and their words to the end of the world. In them hath He set a tabernacle for the sun, Which is as a bridegroom coming out of his chamber, and rejoiceth as a strong man to run a race. His going forth is from the end of the heaven, and his circuit unto the ends of it: and there is nothing hid from the heat thereof.

—Ps. 19:1

Ye are blessed of the Lord which made heaven and earth.

—Ps. 115:15

By the word of the Lord were the heavens made; and all the host of them by the breath of his mouth. For he spake, and it was *done;* he commanded, and it stood fast.

—Ps. 33:6, 9

For all the gods of the nations *are* idols: but the Lord made the heavens.

—Ps. 96:5

My help cometh from the Lord, which made heaven and earth.

—Ps. 121:2

Our help is from the Lord which made heaven and earth.

—Ps. 124:8

The Lord that made heaven and earth bless thee out of Zion.

—Ps.134:3

To Him that by wisdom made the heavens: for His mercy endureth forever.

—Ps. 136:5

Happy is *he* that *hath* the God of Jacob for his help, whose hope is in the LORD his God: Which made heaven, and earth, the sea, and all that therein is: which keepeth truth for ever.

—Ps. 146:5, 6

Testimony of Isaiah

O LORD of hosts, God of Israel, that dwellest between the cherubims, thou art the God, even thou alone, of all the kingdoms of the earth: thou hast made heaven and earth.

—Isa. 37:16

Lift up your eyes on high, and behold who hath created these things, that bringeth out their host by number: he calleth them all by names by the greatness of his might, for that he is strong in power; not one faileth.

—Isa. 40:26

Thus saith God the LORD, He that created the heavens, and stretched them out; He that spread forth the earth, and that which cometh out of it; He the giveth breath unto the people upon it, and spirit to them that walk therein.

—Isa. 42:5

I have made the earth, and created man upon it: I, *even* my hands, have stretched out the heavens, and all their host have I commanded.

—Isa. 45:12

For thus saith the LORD that created the heavens; God himself that formed the earth and made it; he hath established it, he created it not in vain, he formed it to be inhabited. I am the Lord; and there is none else.

—Isa. 45:18

The Testimony of Jeremiah

He hath made the earth by his power, he hath established the world by his wisdom, and hath stretched out the heavens by his discretion.

—Jer. 10:12

I have made the earth, the man and the beast that *are* upon the ground, by my great power and by my outstretched arm, and have given it unto whom it seemed meet unto me.

—Jer. 27:5

Ah Lord God! behold, thou hast made the heaven and the earth by thy great power and stretched out arm, and there is nothing too hard for thee.

—Jer. 32:17

Testimony of Amos

"*Seek* Him that maketh the seven stars and Orion…. The LORD is his name."

—Amos 5:8

Testimony of John

In the beginning was the Word, and the Word was with God, and the Word was God. The same was in the beginning with God. All things were made by him; and without him was not any thing made that was made.

—John 1:1–3

And the Word was made flesh, and dwelt among us….

—John 1:14

Thou art worthy, O Lord, to receive glory and honor and power: for thou hast created all things, and for thy pleasure they are and were created.

—Rev 4:11

And I saw another angel fly in the midst of heaven, having the everlasting gospel to preach unto them that dwell on the earth, and to every nation, and kindred, and tongue, and people. Saying with a loud voice, Fear God, and give glory to him; for the hour of his judgment is come: and worship him that made heaven, and earth, and the sea, and the fountains of waters.

—Rev. 14:6, 7

And sware by him that liveth for ever and ever, who created heaven, and the things that therein are, and the earth, and the things that therein are, and the sea and the things which are therein, that there should be time no longer.

—Rev. 10:6

Saying with a loud voice, Fear God, and give glory to Him; for the hour of His judgment is come: and worship Him that made heaven, and earth, and the sea, and the fountains of waters.

—Rev. 14:7

Testimony of the Apostle Paul

And saying, Sirs, why do ye these things? We also are men of like passions with you, and preach unto you that ye should turn from these vanities unto the living God, which made heaven, and earth, and the sea, and all things that are therin.

—Acts 14:15

For the invisible things of Him from the creation of the world are clearly seen, being understood by the things that are made, *even* His eternal power and Godhead; so that they are without excuse.

—Rom. 1:20

For God, who commanded the light to shine out of darkness, hath shined in our hearts, to give the light of the knowledge of the glory of God in the face of Jesus Christ.

—2 Cor. 4:6

And to make all *men* see what is the fellowship of the mystery, which from the beginning of the world hath been hid in God, who created all things through Jesus Christ....

—Eph. 3:9

Who is the image of the invisible God, the firstborn of every creature: For by Him were all things created, that are in heaven, and that are in earth, visible and invisible, whether *they be* thrones, or dominions, or principalities, or powers: all things were created by him, and for him: And he is before all things, and by him all things consist.

—Col. 1:15–17

God who at sundry times and in diverse manners spake in time past unto the fathers by the prophets, Hath in these last days spoken unto us by *His* Son, whom he hath appointed heir of all things, by whom also he made the worlds; Who being the brightness of *His* glory, and the express image of His person, and upholding all things by the word of his power, when He had by Himself purged our sins, sat down on the right hand of the Majesty on high.

—Heb. 1:1–3

And, Thou, Lord, in the beginning hast laid the foundation of the earth; and the heavens are the works of thine hands.

—Heb. 11:3

Through faith we understand that the worlds were framed by the word of God, so that things which are seen were not made of things which do appear.

—Heb 1:10

1 Ellen G. White, *Testimonies*, vol. 8, Boise, Idaho: Pacific Press Publishing Association, 1948, pp. 258, 259.
2 James Weldon Johnson, *God's Trombones,* The Viking Press, Inc, 1997.

CHAPTER THREE

Before the Beginning

The Eternal Nature of the Godhead

This chapter must of necessity be very brief because our knowledge of "Before the Beginning" must be restricted to the limited amount of information that is revealed in the Scriptures. Let us begin by pondering the question "Who was there?" or "What was there?" before "In the beginning…" There are several texts in the Bible that speak of the eternal nature of God and His existence before the creation of the universe. In commenting on Genesis 1:1, Matthew Henry, the noted Biblical commentator, wrote, "Before the beginning of time there was none but that infinite Being that inhabits eternity…."[1]

The book of Exodus reveals the sacred name of God and His eternal existence. "And Moses said unto God, Behold, *when* I come unto the children of Israel, and shall say unto them, The God of your fathers hath sent me unto you; and they shall say unto me, What *is* his name? What shall I say unto them? And God said unto Moses, I AM THAT I AM: and he said, Thus shalt thou say unto the children of Israel, I AM hath sent me unto you (Exod. 3:13–14).

Moses' encounter with the Most High God at the burning bush not only evidences the existence of God but also reveals God's true nature. When God referred to himself as I AM THAT I AM, God was not only giving Moses another name for Himself (God), but God was revealing to all mankind that He was the eternal, self-existent One. According to Matthew Henry, this name implies:

1. That He is self-existent; He has His being of Himself, and has no dependence upon any other.
2. That He is eternal and unchangeable.
3. That we cannot by searching find Him out.[2]

The noted Christian apologist, Ravi Zacharias, speaks of God as "the only entity that exists, whose reason for His existence is within Himself."

Moses, the author of the first five books of the Bible, and the putative author of the book of Job, is also the author of the nineti-eth division of the Psalms. In this Psalm, he speaks majestically and eloquently of the existence of God before the creation of the universe. "LORD, thou hast been our dwelling place in all generations. Before the mountains were brought forth, or ever thou hadst formed the earth and the world, even from everlasting to everlasting, thou *art* God" (Ps. 90:1, 2).

Likewise Moses in his farewell to the children of Israel reminded them of the eternal nature of God: "The eternal God *is thy* refuge, and underneath *are* the everlasting arms..." (Deut. 33:27). And Solomon, the wisest man that ever lived, beautifully describes the preexistence of the second person of the Godhead:

The Lord possessed me in the beginning of His way, before His works of old. I was set up from everlasting, from the beginning, or ever the earth was. When there were no depths, I was brought forth; when there were no fountains abounding with water. Before the moun-tains were settled, before the hills was I brought forth: while as yet He had not made the earth, nor the fields, nor the highest part of the dust of the world. When He prepared the heavens, I was there: when He set a compass upon the face of the depth: When He established the clouds above: when He strengthened the fountains of the deep: When He gave to the sea His decree, that the waters should not pass His commandment: when He appointed the foundations of the earth:

Then I was by Him, as one brought up with Him: and I was daily his
delight, rejoicing always before Him....

—Prov. 8:22–30

It should be noted that Proverbs 8:22–30 is an allegory in which
wisdom, an attribute of God, is being personified. "Therefore these
verses should not be interpreted as a direct description of Christ" (SDA
Bible Commentary, 972-973).

The prophet Isaiah also describes the everlasting nature of the second person of the Godhead. "For unto us a child is born, unto us a son
is given: and the government shall be upon his shoulder: and his name
shall be called Wonderful, Counselor, The mighty God, The everlasting
Father, The Prince of Peace" (Isa. 9:6). Let us note that Isaiah is careful
to state that the child was born, but the son was given. The Son always
existed. Also in Isaiah 57, the prophet speaks of God as inhabiting eternity: "For thus saith the high and lofty One that inhabiteth eternity,
whose name *is* Holy; I dwell in the high and holy *place,* with him also
that is of a contrite and humble spirit, to revive the spirit of the humble,
and to revive the heart of the contrite ones" (Isa. 57:15).

The prophet Micah in prophesying the place where the Christ child
was to be born, specifically mentions the eternal nature of the second
person of the Godhead. "But thou, Bethlehem Ephratah, *though* thou
be little among the thousands of Judah, yet out of thee shall he come
forth unto me *that* is to be ruler in Israel; whose goings forth *have been
from* of old, from everlasting" (Mic. 5:2).

Perhaps the most revealing and definitive statement in the Bible
concerning the existence of God before the beginning is the text found
in John 1:1–3:

When the world began, the *Word* was already there. The Word was
with *God,* and the nature of the *Word* was the same as the nature of
God. (William Barclay)

When all things began, the Word already was. (New English Bible)

Before the world was created, the Word already existed; he was with
God, and he was the same as God. (Pathfinder Bible)

Before anything else existed, there was Christ. He has always been alive and is himself God. (The Living Bible Paraphrased)

In the beginning [before all time] was the Word [Christ], and the Word was with God, and the Word was God Himself. He was present originally with God. All things were made and came into existence through Him; and without Him was not even one thing made that has come into being. (Amplified Bible)

Jesus, in his valedictory prayer to His Father, made the following significant request: "And now, O Father, glorify thou me with thine own self with the glory which I had with thee before the world was" (John 17:5).

In his epistle to the Colossians, the apostle Paul underscores the existence of Christ before the universe was created. "Who is the image of the invisible God, the firstborn of every creature: For by Him were all things created, that are in heaven, and that are in earth, visible and invisible, whether they *be* thrones, or dominions, or principalities, or powers: all things were created by Him, and for Him: And He is before all things and by him all things consist" (Col. 1:15–17). Also in the book of Hebrews, the apostle Paul speaks of the eternal existence of Christ. "Jesus Christ the same yesterday, and today, and for ever" (Heb. 13:8). In his epistles to the Ephesians and to Timothy, the apostle Paul speaks of the preexistence of the plan of salvation in Christ: "According as he hath chosen us in him before the foundation of the world, that we should be holy and without blame before him in love" (Eph. 1:4). "Who hath saved us, and called us with a holy calling, not according to our works, but according to his own purpose and grace, which was given us in Christ Jesus before the world began" (2 Tim.1:9).

Likewise the apostle Peter speaks of the preappointment of a Savior before the foundation of the world: "Who verily was foreordained before the foundation of the world, but was manifest in these last times for you" (1 Pet. 1:20). Thus the Bible teaches that before the creation of the universe, a transcendent, omnipotent, omniscient, and omnipresent Creator-God existed.

---

1   Matthew Henry, *Commentary on the Whole Bible* (in one volume), Grand Rapids: Zondervan Publishing House, 1960, p. 1.

2   Matthew Henry, p. 75

CHAPTER FOUR

Understanding the First Chapter of Genesis

Biblical Cosmology

The Genesis Account of Creation

If one accepts the credibility of the Bible as validated and substantiated by so many amazing and accurately fulfilled prophecies, then the testimony of the Bible concerning God, the origin of the universe, and man's existence in the cosmos cannot be ignored.

Even though the Bible speaks authoritatively about the origin of the universe by fiat creation and creation ex nihilo, it should be understood that the Bible was not written as a scientific paper or a scientific textbook. The Bible was not written specifically for a scientific audience. When Moses wrote the book of Genesis, he was endeavoring to communicate the story of creation to humble believers in a Creator-God. By faith, creationists accept the Genesis view of creation without reservations.

Note that some believe the Hebrew language is the oldest human language. It is believed to have been divinely structured and was the language of the patriarchs from Adam to Noah, Shem, Ham and Japheth. Whereas the English language contains approximately one million words, the Hebrew language contains only about three thousand. Therefore, the definition and meaning of an Hebrew word must be determined by its contextual use.

The English translation of the first chapter of Genesis presented below is taken from the King James Version. Numbers in parenthesis to the right of certain key words correspond with the numbers of the definition of the equivalent Hebrew term. Lexical definitions are taken from four different sources as listed in reference 1.[1] This chapter is of crucial and paramount importance because the misunderstanding and the misinterpretation of it is responsible for many of the controversial biblical views of the origin of the universe.

Pre Day One

Creation of the Universe Including Terrestrial Matter
Genesis 1:1–2

"In the beginning God (1) created (2) the heaven (3) and the earth (4)" (v.1).

Definitions:

1. (God) [4] *'Elohim'* (plural of *'eloah'*): "the deity; the supreme Being; the true God—a compound word composed of El (the strong one), and *Alah* (to bind oneself by an oath); hence, *Elohiym* is the mighty and faithful one—a uni-plural noun; thus *Elohiym* latently implies the Trinity—the only name used for God in Genesis 1; this name is used about 2,500 times in the Old Testament."[1]

2. (Created) *'Bara'*: "bring forth something; produce that which is new; extraordinary, and/or epochal; produce through supernatural activity. God is always the subject of this verb." "The Hebrew word used for creation, *barah*, is the only word in the Hebrew language that means the creation of something from nothing."[2]

3. (Heaven) *shemeh*: "whenever *shamayim* is used with the eret (earth), as in 1:1, the combination refers to the entire physical universe."

4. (Earth) *'eres*: "the planet earth; a land, a country, or a continent; lands, countries, kingdoms, or regions."

Commentary:

In 2 Peter 3:5, the apostle Peter provides us with his inspired understanding of the creation of heaven and earth. "For they willfully overlook *and* forget this [fact], that the heavens [came into] existence long ago by the word of God, and an earth also which was formed out of water and by means of water." Likewise the writer of Hebrews affirms the creation of terrestrial matter in the beginning. "And, Thou, Lord, in the beginning hast laid the foundation of the earth; and the heavens are the works of thine hands" (Heb. 1:10).

Based on the definitions of the Hebrew words in Genesis 1:1, a more accurate version of Genesis 1:1 should read: In the beginning the Triune God created the universe, including the earth, out of nothing.

"And the earth(4) was without form(5), and void(6); and darkness *was* upon the face of the deep(7). And the spirit(8) of God(1) moved(9) upon the face of the waters."

—Gen. 1:2

Definitions:

5. (Without form; formless) *toho*: "desolate; worthless; wasteness; useless; incapable of being utilized; unformed."
6. (Void; empty) *bohu*: "empty; void; devoid of existence."
7. (Deep) *tehom*: "a great mass of water; the oceans and the seas."
8. (Spirit) *ruah*: "spirit breath; wind–conjunction with Elohim refers to the Holy Spirit."
9. (Moved; hovered) *rahap*: "to brood over, cherishing and vivifying; to be tenderly affected; to be moved."

Commentary:

The Amplified Version of Genesis 1:2 is very descriptive: "The earth was without form and an empty waste, and darkness was upon the face of the very great deep. The Spirit of God was moving (hovering, brooding), over the face of the waters."

The Genesis Gap

Supporting Statement

There was an obvious *gap* between the events described in verses one and two and the beginning of creation week as described in verse three. It should be noted that the six days of creation week are all punctuated with the expression, "let there be...." This marks off creation week from the period of time that preceded it.

The Gap Theory

According to this theory, it is believed by many scholars that Genesis 1:1–2 describe events that predated the first day of earth's creation week. Others postulate that the earth was initially created in the state ("without form and void") ages before creation week. The best interpretation of Scripture and the irrefutable evidences of science support this theory.

Events of Creation Week

Day One—Creation of Light
Genesis 1:3–5

"And God(1) said, Let there be(10) light: and there was light" (v. 3).

Definition:

10. (Let there be) *haya*: "become (when coupled with the Hebrew preposition *l*) cause to appear or arise; cause to be made or done; come into existence; come to pass; make into some thing."

Commentary:

Light is sometimes referred to as the first element of creation. [According to big bang cosmology, light, which is a form of energy and electromagnetic radiation, was created at the moment of the big bang.] This light was spoken into existence by Him who dwelleth "... in the light which no man can approach unto..." (1 Tim. 6:16). "For God, who commanded the light to shine out of darkness, hath shined in our hearts…" (2 Cor. 4:6).

Inspiration is silent concerning the nature, location, and position of this light source. What is known is that this light source performed a function similar to that of the sun's rays. It is believed that this light was of a diffuse nature, dispelling the darkness that previously enveloped the terrestrial sphere while illuminating half of the surface of the earth. As an adjunct to the creation of light on this earth, God instituted the evening and morning cycle, which constitutes an earth day of twenty-four hours. It is wonderful to note that the Creator in His wisdom chose to begin the acts of the creation week with the creation of an entity that is crucial for the existence of most living organisms.

"And God(1) saw the light, that *it was* good: and God divided the light from the darkness. And God(1) called the light Day(11), and the darkness he called Night. And the evening(12) and the morning(13) were the first day(11)" (vv. 4–5).

Definitions:

11. (Day) *yôm*: "sunrise to sunset; sunset to sunset; a space of time (defined by an associated term); an age; time or period (without any reference to solar days)."
12. (Evening) *'ereb*: "the beginning of darkness; dusk, twilight or nightfall; closing; ending; or completion."
13. (Morning) *boqer*: "the breaking forth of light; dawn; day break, or morning; dawning; beginning or origin."

Commentary:

The Hebrew word *yôm* is an excellent example of how the meaning of a Hebrew term is dependent upon its context. The different definitions given above for *yôm* have provided the basis for significant variations in the interpretations of Genesis 1:5–31. However, the strict application of the grammatical rules in Hebrew restricts the meaning of *yôm* in these verses to that of a twenty-four-hour literal day. The noted biblical linguist, Dr. Gerhard Hasel, is unequivocal on this point. "The cumulative evidence, based on comparative, literary, linguistic and other considerations, converges on every level, leading to the singular conclusion that the designation *yôm*, "day," in Genesis 1 means consistently a literal twenty-four-hour day."[3]

Note the rendering of this text in the Amplified Version: "And God called the light Day, and the darkness he called Night. And there was evening, and there was morning, one day."

Day Two—Firmament (Atmospheric Heaven)
Genesis 1:6–8

"And God(1) said, Let there be(10) a firmament(14) in the midst of the waters, and let it divide the waters from the waters. And God(1) made(15) the firmament,(14) and divided the waters which *were* under the firmament(14) from the waters which *were* above the firmament: and it was so. And God(1) called the firmament(14) Heaven(3). And the evening(12) and the morning(13) were the second day(11)" (vv. 6–8).

Definitions:
14. (Firmament; Expanse) *raqia*: "(apparently) visible dome of the sky; (technically the atmosphere immediately above the surface of the earth)."
15. (Made) *'asa*: "produce; manufacture; fabricate."

Commentary:
It should be noted that the writer of Genesis 1:7 did not use the Hebrew term *Bara* (to create out of nothing) but rather the Hebrew term *asa* (to produce, manufacture, fabricate). Once again we see that the events of day two did not represent creation ex nihilo.

From the Hebrew lexicon, it is clear that the Hebrew word for firmament or expanse refers to the atmospheric heaven in Genesis 1:6. In these texts we are given a description of the creation of what is generally called the atmospheric heavens or the atmosphere. In the Bible, this is sometimes referred to as the first heaven. The second heaven is considered to be the starry heaven. And the third is understood to be paradise, the habitation of the Most High God. Note the expression used by the apostle Paul:

I knew a man in Christ above fourteen years ago, (whether in the body, I cannot tell; or whether out of the body, I cannot tell: God knoweth;) such an one caught up to the third heaven. And I knew such a man, (whether in the body, or out of the body, I cannot tell: God knoweth;) How that he was caught up into paradise, and heard unspeakable words, which it is not lawful for a man to utter.

—2 Cor. 12:2–4

Day Three—Seas, Dry Land, and Vegetation
Genesis 1:9–13

"And God(1) said, Let the waters under the heaven(3) be(10) gathered together unto one place, and let the dry *land* appear(16) and it was so. And God(1) called the dry *land* earth; and the gathering together of the waters called he Seas: and God(1) saw that *it was* good. And God(1) said, Let the earth bring forth(17) grass,(18) the herb yielding(19) seed(20), *and* the fruit tree(21) yielding fruit(22) after his kind(23), whose seed(20) *is* in itself, upon the earth: and it was so. And the earth brought forth(17) grass(18), *and* herb yielding(19) seed(20)after his kind(23), and the tree(21) yielding fruit(22), whose seed(20) *was* in itself, after his kind(23): and God saw that *it was* good. And the evening(12) and the morning(13) were the third day(11)" (vv. 9–13).

Definitions:

16. (Appear) *ra' a*: "be seen; appear; show forth, cause one to see; to be perceived or beheld; to be considered."
17. (Bring forth, produce) *dasha*: "to bring forth herbage; to sprout; to bring forth."
18. (Grass, vegetation) *deshe*: "new vegetation; young plants."
19. (Herb yielding, plant bearing) *'eseb*: "green plant(s)."
20. (Seed) *zera*: "embryos of plants, trees, etc., i.e., the embryos of any plant species."
21. (Trees) *'es*: "any large plant containing woody fiber."
22. (Fruit) *peri*: "food and/or embryos produced by any living thing."
23. (Kind) *min*: "species; life form."

Commentary:

The Hebrew tells us that the events of day three represented a bringing forth of seeds, dry land, and vegetation. The third day witnessed the separation of water from land and the appearance of luscious vegetation capable of reproducing itself. The noted Bible commentator E.G. White beautifully describes the appearance and physiography of the earth at the close of the third day of creation week:

> As the earth came forth from the hand of the Maker, it was exceedingly beautiful. Its surface was diversified with mountains, hills, and plains, interspersed with noble rivers and lovely lakes; but the hills and mountains were not abrupt and rugged, abounding in terrific steeps and frightful chasms, as they now do; the sharp, ragged edges of earth's rocky framework were buried beneath the fruitful soil, which everywhere produced a luxuriant growth of verdure. There were no loathsome swamps or barren deserts. Graceful shrubs and delicate flowers greeted the eye at every turn. The heights were crowned with trees more majestic than any that now exist. The air, untainted by foul miasma, was clear and healthful. The entire landscape outvied in beauty the decorative grounds of the proudest palace. The angelic host viewed the scene with delight, and rejoiced at the wonderful works of God.[4]

Day Four—Sun, Moon and Stars
Genesis 1:14–19

"And God(1) said, Let there be(10) lights(24) in the firmament(14) of the heaven(3) to divide the day(11) from the night; and let them be for signs(25), and for seasons, and for days(11), and years: And let them be(10) for lights(24) in the firmament(14) of the heaven(3) to give light upon the earth(4): and it was so. And God(1) made(15) two great lights(24); the greater light(24) to rule the day(11), and the lesser light(24) to rule the night: *he made(*15) the stars also. And God(1) set(26) them in the firmament(14) of the heaven(3) to give light upon the earth(4), And to rule over the day(11) and over the night, and to divide the light from the darkness: and God(1) saw that *it was* good. And the evening(12) and the morning(13) were the fourth day(11)" (vv.14–19).

Definitions:

24. (Lights) *ma'or:* "a luminous body; brightness."
25. (Signs) *'ot:* "signal, measuring mark; token, omen, evidence."
26. (Set) *natan:* "cause to appear."

Commentary:

Once again the Hebrew word *asa* is being used as it was used in verse seven to describe a process of fabrication rather than creation. Opinions concerning the events of day one and day four of creation week have always been controversial. Theologians and theistic scientists have speculated on the following questions: What was the source and nature of the light that was created on day one of creation week? Were the sun, moon, and stars created on day four or did God merely make them visible on day four? In his book, *The Creator and His Workshop,* Dr. R.E. Hoen argues: "Several scriptures which refer to this same creative act of causing the heavenly bodies to appear through the firmament employ the words *prepare, appoint, ordain, and ordinance* rather than the term *create.* All of the organizational activities of the first week of earth were definitely creative, most of them consisting of uniquely fashioning the world and the things therein and thereupon from the materials which the Creator Himself brought into existence at the outset.[5]

In harmony with this view expressed by Dr. Hoen, it is interesting to note that the events of day three (the formation of the seas and dry lands), did not represent creation ex nihilo. Therefore on day four of creation week God could merely have caused these heavenly bodies to appear or to become visible to prospective earth creatures as they are today.

In his book, *Creation—Accident or Design?,* Dr. H.G. Coffin of the Geoscience Research Institute states, "A reading of Genesis 1:14 to 19 conveys the distinct impression that God created the sun, moon, and stars on the fourth day. However, we can hardly include the stars, for this would imply the creation of at least the visible universe at that time…. The twinkling rays of distant stars would not yet have reached us (at the present speed of light) unless they were created long previous to creation week."[6] Frank Lewis Marsh makes this same point in his book, *Studies in Creationism*: "The fact that many stars are millions of light years away from our earth and are yet shedding their light upon us, demonstrates that they have been in existence many many times 6,000."[7] Note that the Hebrew word *natan* explicitly means "cause to appear." This is in harmony with Dr. Hoen's position stated above.

Day Five—Fishes and Fowls
Genesis 1:20–23

"And God(1) said, Let the waters bring forth abundantly the moving creature(27) that hath life, and fowl *that* may fly above the earth(4) in the open firmament(14) of the heaven(3). And God(1) created(2) great whales(28), and every living(29) creature(27) that moveth(29), which the waters brought forth abundantly, after their kind(23), and every winged fowl after his kind(23): and God(1) saw that *it was* good. And God(1) blessed them, saying, Be(10) fruitful, and multiply, and fill the waters in the seas, and let fowl multiply in the earth(4). And the evening(12) and the morning(13) were the fifth day(11)" (vv. 20–23).

Definitions:
27. (Creatures) *sheres*: "swarm of small or minute animals."
28. (Great whales, great creatures) *tanniym*: "great or large sea animal; monster."
29. (Living) *nepesh*: "vital animals, i.e., animals that clearly manifest the soulish attributes of mind, will, and emotion."

Day Six—Land Animals and Man
Genesis 1:24–31

"And God(1) said, Let the earth bring forth(17) the living creature(27) after his kind(23), cattle(30), and creeping thing(31), and beast(32) of the earth after his kind(23): and it was so" (v. 24).

Definitions:
30. (Cattle, livestock) *behemot*: "large land quadruped."
31. (Creeping thing, creatures that move) *remes*: "rapidly moving vertebrates; rodents and/or reptiles."

32. (Beast, animals) *hay:* "wild animals; a multitude or mob; that which is lively or fresh."

"And God(1) made(14) the beast(32) of the earth after his kind(23) and cattle(30) after their kind(23), and everything that creepeth(31) upon the earth after his kind(23): and God(1) saw that *it was* good. And God(1) said, Let us make(15) man(33) in our image, after our likeness: and let them have dominion over the fish of the sea, and over the fowl of the air, and over the cattle(30), and over all the earth, and over every creeping(31) thing that creepeth upon the earth" (vv. 25–26).

Definition:

33. (Man) *'adam:* "human being; the human race; i.e., animals that clearly manifest spirit attributes. Note: there is no evidence for a spirit dimension for the pre-Adamic hominids."

Commentary:

This day witnessed the appearance of land animals and the creation of man—"the crowning act of creation." The psalmist David states, "For thou hast made him a little lower than the angels, and hast crowned him with glory and honour" (Ps. 8:5). And Shakespeare in *Hamlet* marvels at the creature called man:

What a piece of work is man! How noble in
reason! How infinite in faculty, in form
and moving! How express and admirable in
action! How like an angel in apprehension!
How like a god! The beauty of the world!
The paragon of animals! And yet, to me what
is this quintessence of dust?"[8]

E.G. White, the noted Bible commentator, writes:

Man was to bear God's image, both in outward resemblance and in character. Christ alone is "the express image" (Heb. 1:3) of the Father; but man was formed in the likeness of God. His nature was in harmony with the will of God. His mind was capable of comprehending divine things. His affections were pure; his appetites and passions were under the control of reason. He was holy and happy in bearing the image of God and in perfect obedience to His will.

As man came forth from the hand of his Creator, he was of lofty stature and perfect symmetry. His countenance bore the ruddy tint of health, and glowed with the light of life and joy. Adam's height was much greater than that of men who now inhabit the earth. Eve was somewhat less in stature, yet her form was noble, and full of beauty. The sinless pair wore no artificial garments; they were clothed with a covering of light and glory, such as the angels wear.[9]

So God(1) created(2) man(33) in his *own* image, in the image of God(1) created(2) he him; male and female created he them. And God(1) blessed them, and God said unto them, Be(10) fruitful, and multiply, and replenish the earth(4), and subdue(34) it: and have dominion over the fish of the sea, and over the fowl of the air, and over every living thing(32) that moveth upon the earth. And God(1) said, Behold, I have given you every herb bearing(19) seed(20), which *is* upon the face of all the earth(4), and every tree, in the which *is* the fruit of a tree yielding seed(20); to you it shall be for meat. And to every beast(32) of the earth(4), and to every fowl of the air, and to everything that creepeth(31) upon the earth wherein *there is* life, *I have given* every green herb(19) for meat: and it was so. And God(1) saw every thing that he had made(15), and, behold, *it was* very good. And the evening(12) and the morning(13) were the sixth day(11)" (vv. 27–31).

Definition:
34. (Subdue) *kabash*: "subject; subdue; subjugate."

Day Seven—The Sabbath
Genesis 2:1–3

"Thus the heavens and earth were finished, and all the host of them. And on the seventh day God ended his work which he had made; and he rested on the seventh day from all his work which he had made. And God blessed the seventh day, and sanctified it: because that in it he had rested from all his work which God created and made" (Gen. 2:1–3).

The Sabbath, which was instituted on the seventh day of creation week, represents imperishable evidence in support of the biblical view of creation. Six thousand years of Sabbath observance testify to the validity of the Genesis account of creation.

Important points to be considered: The first two verses of Genesis 1 describe the creation of the universe including terrestrial matter. There was an obvious gap between the events described in verses one and two and the beginning of creation week as described in verse three. It should be noted that the six days of creation week are all punctuated with the expression, "let there be." This marks off creation week from the period of time that preceded it.

The six days mentioned in the fourth commandment of the Decalogue refer to the creative events of creation week. "For in six days the Lord made heaven and earth, the sea, and all that in them is, and rested the seventh day: wherefore the Lord blessed the Sabbath day, and hallowed it" (Exod. 20:11). "The heaven" in this commandment refers to the atmospheric heavens created on the second day of creation week; "the earth" and "the seas" refers to the dry land and the seas created on the third day of creation week, and "all that in them is" refers to the fishes, et cetera, created on the fifth day of creation week. Thus we see that the fourth commandment speaks specifically about the creative events that took place on the second, third, and fifth days of creation week. Therefore, "the six days" of the fourth commandment apply to the six days of creation week rather than the time period for the creation of the universe.

The Literal Days of Creation Week

There are those who believe that the days of creation represented long geological eras rather than literal days of twenty-four hours each. However, the Bible is unmistakably clear on this point. The Creator Himself, speaking through Moses, clearly defined the time period of these days by repeating six times in succession that "the evening and the morning" were a particular day. After six days of creative activity, God rested or ceased from this activity on the seventh day and thus instituted the beginning of the weekly cycle of time. Each cycle would end with the seventh-day Sabbath. It is interesting to note that there is an astronomical basis for the day, the month, and the year. However, there is no astronomical basis for the period of time we call a week. In astronomy, a day is defined as the amount of time (twenty-four hours) that it takes for the earth to make a complete rotation on its axis. A lunar month (29.5 days) is defined as the amount of time it takes for the moon to make a complete revolution around the earth. A year is defined as the amount of time (365 days, 5 hours, 48 minutes, and 46 seconds) that it takes for the earth to make a complete revolution around the sun. As a result of the relative positions of the earth, the moon, and the sun, the moon appears to pass through the following four phases: new moon, first quarter, full moon, and last quarter. The period of time it takes the moon to move from one phase to another is incommensurable with the period of time known as a week. In fact, the period of time between phases is not constant since, according to Kepler's Laws, the moon travels fastest when it is closest to the earth at perigee, and slowest when it is farthest from the earth at apogee. Thus we see there is no astronomical basis for the period of time known as a week. God, Himself, marked off this period of time with the institution of the seventh-day Sabbath.

Scholarly analysis of the biblical text used in Genesis 1 is very strong in support of the literal twenty-four hour days of creation week. Concerning the literal days of creation week, Dr. Gerhard Hasel, late professor of Old Testament at Andrews University, stated the following in a paper prepared for presentation at a conference sponsored by the Geoscience Research Institute:

> This paper investigated the meaning of creation "days." It has considered key arguments in favor of a   figurative, non-literal meaning of the creation "days." It found them to be wanting on the basis of genre investigation, literary considerations, grammatical study, syntactical usages, and semantic connections. The cumulative evidence, based on   comparative, literary, linguistic and other considerations

converges on every level, leading to the singular conclusion that the designation *yôm,* "day," in Genesis 1 means consistently a literal twenty-four-hour day.

The author of Genesis 1 could not have produced more comprehensive and all-inclusive ways to express the idea of a literal "day" than the ones that were chosen. There is a complete lack of indicators from prepositions, qualifying expressions, construct phrases, semantic-syntactical connections, and so on, on the basis of which the designation "day" in the creation week could be taken to be anything different than a regular twenty-four-hour day. The combinations of the factors of articular usage, singular gender, semantic-syntactical constructions, time boundaries, and so on, corroborated by the divine promulgations in such Pentateuchal passages of Exodus 20:8–11 and Exodus 31:12–17, suggest uniquely and consistently that the creation "day" is meant to be literal, sequential, and chronological in nature."[3]

Before Dr. Hasel could present this paper, he was tragically killed in August 1994 in an automobile accident while attending this conference at Ogden, Utah. However, this paper was later distributed to the conference attendees.

---

1   Hugh Ross, *The Genesis Question,* (Colorado Springs, Colorado: NavPress Publishing Group, 1998), pp.193–196. Lexical definitions sighted by Hugh Ross:

   a)   R. Laird Harris, Gleason L. Archer, and Bruce K. Waltke, *Theological Workbook of the Old Testament,* vols. 1 & 2 (Chicago: Moody, 1980).

   b)   William Gesenius, *Gesenius' Hebrew-Chaldee Lexicon to the Old Testament* (Grand Rapids, Mich.: Baker, 1979).

   c)   Francis Brown, S. R. Driver, and Charles A. Briggs, *A Hebrew and English Lexicon of the Old Testament* (Oxford, UK: Clarendon Press, 1968).

   d)   James Strong, "A Concise Dictionary of the Words in the Hebrew Bible," *in Strong's Exhaustive Concordance of the Bible* (McLean, Va.: MacDonald Publishing).

2   Gerald L. Schroeder. *Genesis and the Big Bang*, New York, NY: Bantam Books 1990, p. 62.
3   Dr. Gerhard Hasel, a published paper that was to be presented at a conference sponsored by the Geoscience Research Institute in August 1994.
4   Ellen G. White, *Patriarchs and Prophets*, Mountain View, CA: Pacific Press Publishing Association, 1913, p. 44.
5   Reu E. Hoen, *The Creator and His Workshop*, Mountain View, CA: Pacific Press Publishing Association, 1951, p. 43.
6   Harold G. Coffin, *Creation—Accident or Design?*, Washington, D.C.: Review and Herald Publishing Association, 1969, p. 27.
7   Frank L. Marsh, *Studies in Creationism*, Lincoln, Nebraska: Union College, 1946, p. 28.
8   William Shakespeare, *The Complete Works, Hamlet*, New York: The Viking Press, 1986, II *ii* 300–304.
9   White, p. 45.

CHAPTER FIVE

In the Beginning

The Beginning of Time

According to Einstein's general theory of relativity, "time and space do not exist independently of the universe or of each other." This means that we live or exist in a space-time continuum. Therefore, time and space were created when the universe was first brought into existence.

Matthew Henry, the noted Bible commentator, states the following concerning the beginning of time: "When this work was produced: In the beginning, that is, in the beginning of time, when that clock was first set agoing: time began with the production of those beings that are measured by time. Before the beginning of time there was none but that infinite Being that inhabits eternity...."[1]

In his book, *The Universe in a Nutshell*, the British mathematical physicist Stephen Hawking discusses Immanuel Kant's "antimony of pure reason" and refuted it. Kant had argued:

If the universe had indeed been created, why had there been an infinite wait before the creation? On the other hand, if the universe had existed forever, why hadn't everything that was going to happen already happened, meaning that history was over? In particular, why hadn't the universe reached thermal equilibrium, with everything at the same temperature? Kant called this problem an 'antimony of pure reason,' because it seemed to be a logical contradiction; it didn't have a resolution. But it was a contradiction only within the context of the Newtonian mathematical model, in which time was an infinite line, independent of what was happening in the universe.[2]

The fallacy in Immanuel Kant's reasoning is that he assumed that time could have an existence apart from the universe.

A Chronology of the Creation of the Universe

The Moment of Creation

When was the moment of creation? When was the "in the beginning"? The Bible is silent concerning the moment of creation, the time of the "in the beginning," but big bang cosmology suggests that the universe was created about 15 billion years ago. This time period is so long that in human terms it approximates an eternity of time. It is equivalent to 15 million life spans of one thousand years each. You will recall that Methuselah, who had the longest life span in biblical history, lived for 969 years.

It seems reasonable to assume that at the moment of creation, a transcendent, omnipotent, omniscient Creator-God created energy, matter, and the dimensions of space and time when He created the universe. By transcendent we mean that He is above, beyond, and outside the universe of energy, matter, space and time. This idea of divine transcendency is alluded to by Solomon in his prayer at the dedication of the temple in Jerusalem. "But will God in very deed dwell with men on the earth? behold, heaven and the heaven of heavens cannot contain thee; how much less this house which I have built!" (2 Chron. 6:18). And the author of Psalms 113 had the transcendency of God in mind when he wrote, "The LORD is high above all nations, *and* his glory above the heavens. Who *is* like unto our God, who dwelleth on high, Who humbleth *himself* to behold *the things that are* in heaven, and in the earth!" (Ps. 113:4–6).

Thus we see that God humbles Himself in the very act of beholding the universe, which He has created. Likewise, the apostle Paul, in his famous speech on Mars' Hill, hinted at the transcendency of God when he said, "God that made the world and all things therein, seeing that he is Lord of heaven and earth, dwelleth not in temples made with hands; Neither is worshipped with men's hands, as though he needed any thing, seeing he giveth to all life, and breath, and all things (Acts 17:24–25).

A Biblical and Scientific Model (Theory) for the Creation of the Universe

The following is a summary of the important postulates in this theory:

1. **Creation of the universe.** At the moment of creation, "in the beginning," an eternal, transcendent, omnipotent, omniscient Creator-God created energy, matter, the dimensions of space and time, and the fundamental forces of physics, which are gravity, electromagnetism, and the color force (the nuclear strong force and the nuclear weak force) when He created the universe.

In addition to the created items mentioned above, the apostle Paul includes the following entities as components of God's creation:

For I am persuaded beyond doubt—am sure—that neither death, nor life, nor angels, nor principalities, nor things impending *and* threatening, nor things to come, nor powers, nor height, nor depth, nor anything else in all creation will be able to separate us from the love of God which is in Christ Jesus our Lord.
—Rom. 8:38–39, AMP

Who is the image of the invisible God, the firstborn of every creature: For by him were all things created, that are in heaven, and that are in earth, visible and invisible, whether *they be* thrones, or dominions, or principalities, or powers: all things were created by him and for him: And he is before all things, and by him all things consist."
—Col. 1:15–17

Supporting statement: "In the beginning, God created the heaven and the earth" (Gen. 1:1). This text refers to the creation of the universe including the starry heaven and terrestrial matter. At the moment of creation all of the cosmic matter (the ninety-two chemical elements) that would become the components of galaxies, stars, and planets came into existence by fiat creation (by command) and creation ex nihilo (out of nothing). Fiat creation is based on Psalm 33:9: "For he spake, and it was done; he commanded and it stood fast." And ex nihilo is based on Hebrews 11:3. "Through faith we understand that the worlds were framed by the word of God, so that things which are seen were not made of things which do appear." (See Chapter 2.)

The heaven mentioned in Genesis 1:1 must refer to the starry heaven since the atmospheric heaven (the firmament) was not created until the second day of creation week. This would also explain why, according to science, the ages of stars approximate the age of the universe. Hebrews 1:10, which is a parallel text to Genesis 1:1, supports this idea: "And, Thou, Lord, in the beginning hast laid the foundation of the earth; and the heavens are the works of thine hands" (Heb. 1:10).

The anthropic principle (see Chapter 6) also supports the idea that all of the matter in the universe was created at the same time.

2. **Formation of galaxies, stars, and planets.** In the course of time the Creator formed the cosmic matter that was created "in the beginning" into galaxies, stars, and planets and habitable worlds.

Supporting statement: Big bang cosmology suggests that the elementary particles created at the time of the big bang condensed to form atomic nuclei, which then formed hydrogen and helium atoms, which later condensed to form galaxies and stars. It has been estimated that the formation of stars and galaxies occurred about 500,000 years after the big bang.[3] It was at this time that the temperature of the universe had cooled sufficiently to permit the formation of atoms by the Coulombic attraction of atomic nuclei for electrons. This crucial formation of atoms could then lead to the formation of stars and galaxies.

The statement in Genesis 1:16, "he made the stars also" was included parenthetically in listing the creative events for the fourth day of creation week. Most Bible commentators agree that on the fourth day of creation week, the sun and moon were made to appear.

In his book, *The Moment of Creation*, James S. Trefil provides an informative account of the cosmological changes that would occur in the universe if we were to travel backward in time from the present to the moment of the big bang:

> The most intriguing thing about the big bang theory is that it tells us that the universe was not always in the state in which we see it now. The stars and the galaxies seem ageless to us, and indeed they are, compared with a single human life or the span of recorded history. But even the "eternal" stars were born at some time in the past, and they will certainly die at some time in the future. The best way to think about the time scale in relation to the birth of the universe is to imagine the entire 15 billion years since the big bang compressed into a single year, which I shall call the galactic year. ...If we imagine moving backward in time through the galactic year, we would see the galaxies (in very much their present form) getting closer and closer together. The effect would be like watching a movie run in reverse. The film would show the same thing all the way from the present (December 31) to within about an hour of the beginning of the galactic year on January 1. It would not be until we had reached the first hour of the galactic year (less than a million years in real time from the big bang) that any change in the universe would become evident. Still watching the film run backward, we would see the galaxies come together into a single undifferentiated mass of atoms. This would be a change, of course, but it would not be fundamental because even though the overall structure of the universe had changed, the basic unit of matter would still be the atom—an electrically neutral object in which as many negatively charged electrons circle the nucleus as there are positively charged protons within the nucleus itself.

> Continuing to press backward in time, we would see this mass of atoms contract and heat up for about half an hour. At this point (about 500,000 years after the big bang in real time), the temperature would be high enough, and collisions between atoms violent enough, that electrons would be torn loose from their nuclei. Atoms

would then cease to exist, and matter would appear in a fundamentally new state, one in which particles of opposite charge are free to move around independently of each other. This state of matter is called a plasma. Plasmas are routinely produced in physics laboratories these days, so we know a good deal about the way matter behaves in this state."[4]

3. **Creation of the angels and other heavenly beings.** Long before the creation of planet earth and man, angels and other heavenly beings were created.

Supporting statement: The Bible is silent concerning the time when the angels and other heavenly beings were created. However, two things are certain. First, the angels and other heavenly beings were created, and second, they were created long before the creation of man. Those who support a young universe theory fail to allow time for the creation of the angels and other heavenly beings. The following texts tell us about the existence of other worlds (planets) inhabited by individuals called "the sons of God":

> Where wast thou when I laid the foundations of the earth? declare, if thou hast understanding. Whereupon are the foundations thereof fastened? or who laid the corner stone thereof; When the morning stars sang together, and all the sons of God shouted for joy?
> —Job 38:4, 6–7

> Now there was a day when the sons of God came to present themselves before the LORD, and Satan came also among them.
> —Job 1:6

These texts reveal that the sons of God are the representatives of other habitable worlds. Satan (who was Lucifer before he fell) considered himself to be the representative of this world.

Speaking of the creation of Lucifer, the prophet Ezekiel wrote:

80

Thou hast been in Eden the garden of God; every precious stone was thy covering…. Thou art the anointed cherub that covereth; and I have set thee so: thou wast upon the holy mountain of God; thou hast walked up and down in the midst of the stones of fire. Thou wast perfect in thy ways from the day that thou wast created, till iniquity was found in thee.

—Ezek. 28:13–15

The book of Job also tells us that heavenly beings were present at the creation of the earth. See Job 38:4, 6–7.

4. **The fall of Lucifer.** Sometime before the creation of planet earth and man, Lucifer was cast out of heaven.

Supporting statement: The Bible is silent concerning the time when Lucifer was cast out of heaven. However, it is believed that this occurred before creation week and the creation of man.

Supporters of the young universe theory fail to allow time for the rebellion and fall of Lucifer as described in Revelation 12:7–9. In his book, *The Creator and His Workshop*, the physical chemist and creationist, Dr. Reu E. Hoen states:

The Creator also brought into existence the material of which the universe is composed, and fabricated many units of it into inhabited worlds. As the Father and the Son laid plans to form the material of this earth into a habitable world and to create man upon it, Lucifer became jealous and started rebellion in heaven. Consequently the plans for the organization and peopling of the earth were halted until the rebellion had ripened into open revolt and Satan and his angels had been cast out of heaven. Thereupon the plans for the completion of the earth were at once consummated."[5]

The prophet Isaiah provides the following picturesque description of the fall of Lucifer:

How art thou fallen from heaven, O Lucifer, son of the morning! How art thou cut down to the ground, which didst weaken the nations! For thou hast said in thine heart, I will ascend into heaven, I will exalt my throne above the stars of God: I will sit also upon the mount of the congregation, in the sides of the north: I will ascend above the heights of the clouds; I will be like the most High. Yet thou shalt be brought down to hell, to the sides of the pit. They that see thee shall narrowly look upon thee, and consider thee, saying, Is this the man that made the earth to tremble, that did shake kingdoms; That made the world as a wilderness, and destroyed the cities thereof; that opened not the house of his prisoners?

—Isa. 14:12–17

And in the book of Revelation we read:

And there was war in heaven: Michael and his angels fought against the dragon; and the dragon fought and his angels, And prevailed not; neither was their place found any more in heaven. And the great dragon was cast out, that old serpent, called the Devil, and Satan, which deceiveth the whole world: he was cast out into the earth, and his angels were cast out with him.

—Rev. 12:7–9

Speaking of the fall of Lucifer, Jesus told his disciples, "I beheld Satan as lightning fall from heaven" (Luke 10:18). Speaking to the Pharisees, Jesus described the debased and depraved state to which Lucifer (the light bearer) had fallen when he became Satan (the enemy): "Ye are of your father the devil, and the lusts of your father ye will do. He was a murderer from the beginning, and abode not in the truth, because there is no truth in him. When he speaketh a lie, he speaketh of his own: for he is a liar, and the father of it" (John 8:44).

5. **Postponement of the creation of planet earth and man.**
   Some Bible commentators believe that the creation of man on planet earth had to be postponed until Lucifer's rebellion had ripened into open revolt.

Supporting statement: In his book, *The Creator and His Workshop*, Dr. Reu E. Hoen states:

As the Father and the Son laid plans to form the material of this earth into a habitable world and to create man upon it, Lucifer became jealous and started rebellion in heaven. Consequently the plans for the organization and peopling of the earth were halted until the rebellion had ripened into open revolt and Satan and his angels had been cast out of heaven. Thereupon the plans for the completion of the earth were at once consummated."[5]

Supporting this scenario, the noted Bible commentator E.G. White states the following:

Then there was war in heaven. The Son of God, the Prince of heaven, and His loyal angels engaged in conflict with the archrebel and those who united with him. The Son of God and true, loyal angels prevailed; and Satan and his sympathizers were expelled from heaven. All the heavenly host acknowledged and adored the God of justice. Not a taint of rebellion was left in heaven. All was again peaceful and harmonious as before. Angels in heaven mourned the fate of those who had been their companions in happiness and bliss. Their loss was felt in heaven. The Father consulted His Son in regard to at once carrying out their purpose to make man to inhabit the earth.[6]

6. **Condition of planet Earth before creation week.** Genesis 1:2 describes the condition of the earth prior to the first day of creation week.

Supporting statement: "And the earth was without form, and void; and darkness was upon the face of the deep. And the Spirit of God moved upon the face of the waters" (Gen. 1:2). This text tells us two things: one, that the cosmic material of the earth before the first day of creation week "was without form, and void," and, two, that water was present. In commenting on Genesis 1:2 in his book, *Creation—Accident or Design?*, Dr. Harold G. Coffin states:

The phrase "without form, and void" is descriptive of the earth's condition at the time the creative acts began to take place—the molding, fashioning, and organization of the earth's surface into a place habitable by man, and the creation of the myriad life forms upon the earth. This expression describes the chaotic state that was changed by successive creative acts during creation week into one of order and beauty.[7]

It is interesting to note that the prophet Jeremiah uses the identical language of Genesis 1:2 to describe the condition of the earth during the millennium: "I beheld the earth, and, lo, it was without form, and void; and the heavens, and they had no light."

—Jer. 4:23

7. **Creation week for planet Earth.** During this week terrestrial matter (without form and void) was organized into a habitable world.

Supporting statement: The fourth commandment of the Decalogue speaks specifically of the creation or organization of the cosmic material into this habitable planet known as Earth. "For *in* six days the LORD made heaven and earth, the sea, and all that in them *is*, and rested the seventh day: wherefore the LORD blessed the Sabbath day, and hallowed it" (Exod. 20:11).

The "heaven" in this commandment refers to the atmospheric heavens created on the second day of creation week; "the earth" and "the seas" refer to the dry land and the seas created on the third day of creation week, and "all that in them is" refers to the vegetation created on the third day and the fishes, et cetera, created on the fifth day of creation week. Thus we see that the fourth commandment speaks specifically about the creative events that took place on the second, the third, and the fifth days of creation week. Therefore, the six days of the fourth commandment represent the six days of creation week rather than the time period for the creation of the universe. The details of creation week are discussed in Chapter 4, "Understanding the First Chapter of Genesis," of this book.

Summary

The theory stated above, which consists of seven postulates, provides an eloquent and harmonious, biblical and scientific account and chronology of the creation of the universe from the moment of creation to creation week for this earth. This theory is consistent with the unequivocal testimony of Scripture and the irrefutable evidences of science (big bang cosmology). (See Chapter 6.)

Those creationists who support the young universe theory usually neglect to allow time for such events as the creation and existence of other worlds, the creation of angels, the creation of the sons of God, and the fall of Lucifer prior to creation week for this earth. They further assume, in spite of irrefutable scientific evidence to the contrary, that the earth and all of the heavenly bodies were created approximately six thousand to ten thousand years ago.

The Big Bang

Hubble's discovery in 1929 of an expanding universe had profound cosmological significance and suggested the concept of the genesis of the universe from a "monstrous, explosive expansion" of a primordial atom. This concept is known as the big bang. From an expanding universe, it is possible to extrapolate backward in time to "zero time" (the moment of the big bang) when the universe was infinitesimally small and had infinite density. Under these conditions all of the laws and theories of science would break down. Mathematicians refer to this condition as a singularity. In cosmology, a singularity is "a point at which space and time are infinitely distorted by gravitational forces."

In 1970 Roger Penrose and Stephen Hawking, two brilliant British mathematical physicists, developed a mathematical proof for the occurrence of a big bang. (See Chapter 6 for a detailed discussion of the big bang.)

A Big-Bang Perspective of a Cosmologist

The following is a summary history of the universe by Stephen Hawking from the time of the big bang to the present time.

...All the mathematical equations can be fitted together to build an astonishingly precise picture of its evolution.

It all begins with a dramatic big bang explosion producing nothing but searing hot energy at first. This energy somehow develops slight variations in its texture and it spreads outward and starts to cool. This allows for slightly hotter spots where, within the first second after the big bang, energy starts converting into particles and anti-particles; and slightly cooler spots which are destined to become the first voids in space. Most of the particles and antiparticles start to be drawn close enough together by gravity for what is known as the electromagnetic force to make them combine; and most of the anti-matter is lost in annihilations, leaving only matter swirling in grow-ing irregular clumps. Until three minutes after the big bang, it is still too hot for these subatomic particles to build anything together; but then some of them start to bind into what will become the nuclei of atoms. It takes 300,000 years for things to cool down enough for electrons to couple with these nuclei to form the first atoms. By then about 20 percent of the nuclei are the heavier type found in helium; the other 80 percent are used to create hydrogen. All the other known chemical elements will evolve much later on.

It takes a billion (1,000,000,000) years, according to all the equa-tions, before millions and millions and millions of these hydrogen and helium atoms have been clumped together by gravity. There are millions of these clumps, each one destined to become a huge cosmic body—typically a whole galaxy. As gravity presses some of these at-oms together more and more tightly, the hydrogen atom begins to fuse in the way Fred Hoyle and his colleagues predicted; stars begin to form within the emerging galaxy and eventually they shine; and the whole life cycle begins, in which all the heavier chemical ele-ments are formed. First hydrogen atoms fuse to produce helium at-oms. Then, as the hydrogen starts to get used up, gravitational pressures increase, and the helium atoms start to fuse. One by one, the heavier elements are produced, each in turn fueling fusion reac-tions to produce the next heaviest element as gravity compresses the star into the denser and denser mass.

Depending on its size, once iron has been formed in the star, it either dies slowly and sheds its elements into space, leaving a white dwarf star, which cools into a brown dwarf (an iron ghost left to wander in space); or the star dies dramatically, exploding in a supernova and creating all the elements heavier than iron in the process. These ele-ments drift through space until they are drawn by gravity into a new heavenly body. If enough matter is pulled in, a new star can be born; but if the fusion reactions do not get started, a planet very like Earth can result.... After 15 billion years the universe has evolved to be the way we see it today.[8]

Stephen Hawking is a brilliant mathematical physicist whom many consider to be the successor to Albert Einstein. He presently holds the position of Lucasian Professor of Mathematics at Cambridge University. This is a position previously held by such illustrious notables as Sir Isaac Newton and Paul A.M. Dirac.

A Big-Bang Perspective of a Creationist

The following is the perspective of a creationist whose views allow for the possibility of a big bang mechanism for the creation of the universe.

The possibility that the big bang theory is the correct physical scenario for what happened in the past remains open. If this were to be indisputably confirmed, what, then, would we make of its time scale of some 15 billion years since the origin of the universe when compared to the biblical time scale of some six thousand years.

I do not see this as an insurmountable problem. A careful reading of the Bible shows that we might well make a difference between the creation of the planet Earth as a cosmic body and the fashioning of our planet as the dwelling place for humankind during creation week. Does not the very first verse of the Bible allow us to place the creation of many things in a distant past called "the beginning"?

This would help us to understand why it is possible to see stars and galaxies that are distances of millions of light-years and whose light could not have reached us if it had begun its cosmic journey only about six thousand years ago. To argue that God created these luminaries with their radiations filling the universe right from the beginning seems a bit contrived. Why should God want to give the impression that the universe is billions of years old if in fact it came into being only about six thousand years ago?

It also gives an answer to the question, What was God doing during the eternity before the creation week? I rather believe He was busy fashioning multitudes of other worlds, and other creatures who lovingly worship Him.

Ellen White did not believe that everything in the universe was created during creation week. She refers to inhabitants of other worlds before Satan's rebellion and to the creation of the earth after his rebellion.

If we understand Genesis and other Bible references to the creation of things as referring only to the origin of life on earth and its immediate habitat, then most, if not all, problems of interpretation vanish and a consistent picture emerges. God created all matter in the very distant past, gave it the present structure we see in the universe through some very energetic processes—maybe, but not necessarily, those that we now refer to as the big bang—started the execution of His plans for this earth about six thousand years ago, and will finish His plans for the world, its inhabitants, and the replenishment of a large number of empty seats in heaven in the very near future.

Meanwhile, "the secret things belong to the Lord our God" (Deut. 29:29 NIV) until such time as we will be able to commune with Him again face-to-face.[9]

Dr. Mart de Groot is an astronomer and director of the Armagh Observatory in Northern Ireland.

---

1   Matthew Henry, *Commentary on the Whole Bible* (in one volume), Grand Rapids: Zondervan, 1960, p. 1.
2   Stephen Hawking, *The Universe in a Nutshell*, New York, NY: Bantum Books, 2001, pp.32–34.
3   James S. Trefil, *The Moment of Creation*, New York: Charles Scribner's Sons, 1983, p.23.
4   James S. Trefil, pp. 21–23.

5   Reu E. Hoen, *The Creator and His Workshop*, Mountain View, CA: Pacific Press Publishing Association, 1951, p. 15.

6   Ellen G. White, *The Story of Redemption*, Hagerstown, MD: Review and Herald Publishing Association, 1947, p. 19.

7   Harold G. Coffin, *Creation—Accident or Design?*, Washington, D.C.: Review and Herald Publishing Association, 1969, p. 20.

8   Stephen Hawking, *Stephen Hawking's Universe: The Cosmos Explained*, New York, NY: Basic Books, 1997, pp. 154–157.

9   Dr. Mart de Groot, "God and the Big Bang", Hagerstown, MD: *Adventist Review*, Aug. 13 1992, vol. 169. p.13.

CHAPTER SIX

Big Bang Cosmology

Science Boldly Goes Where No One Has Gone Before

N ote to the reader: This chapter traces the history of scientific thought for a period of two thousand years, that culminated in the discovery of an expanding universe and the genesis of big bang cosmology.

Greek Science—The Journey Begins

It may be said that man's journey to a rational understanding of the anatomy of the universe began with the contributions of Greek science. Centuries before Columbus' voyage to the new world, Greek science had firmly established that the earth was round and not flat. Their conclusion was based on the following observations: First, it was noted that during eclipses of the moon, the shadow of the earth on the moon was round. Second, it was observed that the altitude of Polaris, the North Star, varies as one moves from north to south or from south to north. At the North Pole, Polaris would be directly overhead, but at the equator it would lie on the horizon. And third, it was common knowledge that one always sees the sail of an approaching ship on the horizon before seeing the hull.

Ptolemy and the Geocentric Theory

About AD 150 the Greek astronomer Ptolemy (*Claudius Ptolemaeus,* Greek astronomer) proposed a cosmological model for the universe. In this model he placed the earth at the center of the universe surrounded by eight spheres – one for the sun, one for the moon, one for each of the five planets known at that time (Mercury, Venus, Mars, Jupiter, and Saturn), and one for the "fixed" stars. The sun, the moon, and each planet traveled in a circle (epicycle) whose center moves along the sphere. Ptolemy's model, though complicated, was successful in providing a reasonable description of the movements of the heavenly bodies. Because this model placed man at the center of the universe in harmony with the anthropocentric theology of the Church, the Church adopted and supported this model of the universe.

Copernicus and the Heliocentric Theory

The Ptolemaic view of the universe held sway for almost fifteen centuries, but all of this would come to an end in 1519 when the Polish priest-scientist, Nicolaus Copernicus (1473–1543) proposed an heliocentric model of the universe with the sun at the center of a solar system and each of the planets (including the earth) traveling around the sun (Greek *helios,* "sun") in circular orbits. Even though the heliocentric model was more elegant than the Ptolemaic model, it did not accurately describe the motions of the planets around the sun. Copernicus recognized that his model was pure heresy and so to avoid persecution, he published it anonymously. He died in 1543 without receiving the proper recognition that was due him.

The Record Keeping of Tycho Brahe

For twenty years, from 1576 to 1597, Tycho Brahe (1546–1601), a Danish astronomer, made consistent and exact observations of the movements of the sun, moon, planets and stars. As a result of these painstaking observations, he was able to compile the first accurate and continuous record keeping of planetary positions. This data would become the basis for Kepler's discoveries of the laws of planetary motion.

Kepler's Laws of Planetary Motion

After the death of Copernicus, Johannes Kepler (1571–1630), a German mathematician and a former assistant of Tycho Brahe, discovered by diligent observation that the planets moved around the sun in ellipses rather than circles. An ellipse looks like an elongated circle. This discovery by Kepler not only revived the heliocentric theory, but marked the demise of the geocentric theory. The heliocentric theory as modified by Kepler was successful in providing an accurate description of the movements of the heavenly bodies.

In addition to placing the heliocentric theory on a firm mathematical and scientific foundation, Kepler also discovered three laws of planetary motion. In fact, Kepler was so enthralled with his discoveries of planetary motion, that he exclaimed "Oh my God, I am thinking Thy thoughts after Thee."

Galileo Galilei—a Giant Is Born

Following the success of the heliocentric theory as modified by Kepler, Galileo Galilei (Italian astronomer and physicist, 1564–1642) was emboldened to publish the ideas of Copernicus. The Church became furious. Galileo was immediately placed under house arrest and ordered to cease his publishing activity. It was during this period of house arrest that Galileo's genius flourished. He discovered the laws of falling bodies and the law of the pendulum. He also constructed a telescope and was the first to use it to study the heavenly bodies. His observation of the four moons revolving around Jupiter convinced him that the Church was wrong in continuing to support the geocentric theory. Immediately after publishing these heretical ideas, he was summoned to Rome, placed on trial, and condemned to death. To avoid being burned at the stake, Galileo recanted and retracted his heretical ideas before the Church's tribunal. However, on leaving the court it is said that he muttered: "The earth still moves. The earth still moves."

Sir Isaac Newton—A Giant on the Shoulders of Giants

It is significant to note that in the year Galileo died, Sir Isaac Newton (mathematical physicist, 1642–1727) was born. Newton continued the scientific dynasty begun by Copernicus, Kepler, and Galileo.

It is said that when Newton entered Cambridge University he picked up four or five books on mathematics to read. Six months later, he was making significant contributions to the field of mathematics and eighteen months later, he was considered to be one of the greatest mathematicians alive. Sir Isaac Newton improved the design of the telescope. He discovered his famous three laws of motion and invented the Calculus. It was Laplace (1749–1827, French astronomer and mathematician) who said of Newton's invention of the Calculus that "it will always remain preeminent above all other productions of the human mind."

However, Newton's greatest contribution to cosmology was his discovery of gravity and the law of universal gravitation. It is believed that the idea of gravity came to Newton while he was in a contemplative mood and observed an apple falling to the ground. The genius of Newton was extraordinary. He recognized that not only was the earth pulling on the apple but that the apple was also pulling the earth to itself. Newton combined his theory of gravity with Kepler's laws of planetary motion and Galileo's laws of motion. By doing this, he was able to accurately describe the movements of the planets in elliptical orbits around the sun. Newton provided science with a mathematical description of a universe that operated with the precision of a mechanical clock. His book, *The Mathematical Principle of Natural Philosophy,* represented a blueprint of a mathematical-mechanical model of the universe.

A significant episode in Newton's life that reveals his humanity, occurred when he had a nervous breakdown and recovered completely. While Newton was serving as Master of the Mint, the Swiss mathematician Jean Bernoulli, prepared two extremely difficult and challenging mathematical problems and sent them to the greatest mathematicians of that time. It is reported that when Newton received his copies of the problems, he worked them immediately before going to bed and sent them back to Bernoulli unsigned. When Bernoulli received Newton's solution, he instantly recognized the style of the author and remarked, "as the lion is known by his claw." Another version of this story has Bernoulli making reference to Newton's recovery from a nervous breakdown by saying, "The lion's paw has healed."

On reflecting upon his lifetime of accomplishments, it is reported that Newton said, "If I have seen further than others it is because I have been able to stand on the shoulders of giants." And in beautiful humility he confessed, "I feel like I have been like a child playing with pebbles on the seashore while the great ocean of truth lay undiscovered before me."

The Telescope and the Spectroscope—Instruments for the Journey

The first rudimentary telescope was invented in Holland and used as a toy. In 1609, Galileo heard of this unusual instrument and secured or constructed one of them for use and studying the heavenly bodies. It was with this telescope that he discovered the four moons revolving about the planet Jupiter. The first significant improvement in the design of the telescope was made by Sir Isaac Newton who replaced one of the lenses with a reflecting concave mirror. Newton's telescope had a five-inch mirror. In contrast, Edwin Hubble used the 100-inch telescope on Mt. Wilson to view, photograph, and study galaxies 500 million light years away. Remember that a light year is the distance that light travels in one year—six trillion miles. The largest terrestrial telescope is the 200-inch telescope on Mt. Palomar.

The effectiveness of a telescope is based on its magnifying and light-gathering ability. When one considers that the pupil of the eye has only an area of 0.03 square inch, it is understandable that the 200-inch telescope on Mt. Palomar with a square area of 31,400 square inches can gather almost one-million times as much light as the unaided eye. Since the maximum magnifying power of a telescope is usually forty times the diameter of its objective, it is evident that the 200-inch telescope on Mt. Palomar has a maximum magnifying power of 8,000.

Spectroscopy is the analysis of light by means of a spectroscope. A spectroscope consists of three important parts: (1) a collimator which makes the entering beam of light parallel, (2) a prism which bends or refracts the parallel rays of light, and (3) a telescope to permit observation of the spectrum.

In the year 1666, Sir Isaac Newton showed that white light is composed of seven "basic colors." He did this by passing a beam of parallel rays of white light through a prism, and observing the emergence of a band of light consisting of the following colors: red, orange, yellow, green, blue, indigo, and violet. A mnemonic device for remembering the order of these colors is the name "Roy G. Biv." This phenomenon occurs because each component of the white light is refracted or bent to a different degree as it passes through the prism. The red component, which has the longest wavelength, is bent the least, and the violet component, which has the shortest wavelength, is bent the most.

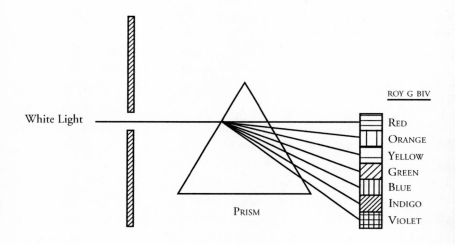

Figure 6.1 The Visible Spectrum

In the decomposition of white light by means of a prism, the band of colored lights that emerges from the prism is called a spectrum. A spectrum is best defined as an ordered separation of light according to wavelength. There are three types of spectra (plural for spectrum): continuous spectrum, bright-line spectrum and dark-line spectrum. A continuous spectrum is one which contains all wavelengths of light (no lines or gaps). Such a spectrum is obtained when the light source is an incandescent solid or a highly compressed gas. The stars (including our sun) and an ordinary electric light bulb are examples of light sources that can produce continuous spectra. A bright-line spectrum is produced when light from an incandescent gas is passed through the prism of a spectroscope. The dark-line spectrum is obtained when light from an incandescent gas passes through a cooler gas of the same element before being analyzed. The lines in a dark line spectrum are also known as Fraunhofer lines. Joseph von Fraunhofer (Bavarian optician and physicist, 1787–1826) is considered to be the father of spectroscopic analysis.

The nursery rhyme, "Twinkle, twinkle, little star, how I wonder what you are," may be good poetry but poor astronomy. By means of a spectroscope it is possible to analyze the light from the sun and from distant stars, and the analysis of this light enables us to identify the chemical elements that are present in these stars. In fact, the element helium (Greek *helios*, "sun") was discovered in the sun before it was discovered on earth. Each chemical element has its own unique atomic structure and therefore its own unique line spectrum. When the electrons in its atoms are energized so that they move up and down, they emit light of definite wavelengths (bright lines). Thus, for each atomic structure, there is a corresponding pattern of lines or wavelengths that represents the "fingerprint" or "signature" of that element. By means of spectroscopic analysis, it is now known that the sun has the same composition as that of all of the other stars in the universe.

The Doppler Effect— "Speedometer" for Storms and Stars

In 1842, Christian Doppler (Christian Johann Doppler, 1803–1853, Austrian physicist) discovered an important principle or effect which is used today to measure the rotation of winds in a tornado as well as to ascertain the movements of galaxies at the edge of the universe.

It is known that light of long wavelength (red) has a low frequency, and light of short wavelength (blue) has a high frequency. The Doppler

Effect illustrates the relationship between the direction of motion of a light source and the frequency of light reaching an observer. When a light source (a star) is moving toward an observer, there is an increase in the number of waves per second (the frequency) reaching the observer. This increase in the frequency (toward shorter wavelength) represents a shift toward the blue region of the spectrum. On the other hand, if a light source is moving away from an observer, the number of waves per second (the frequency) reaching the observer decreases.

This decrease in the frequency (toward longer wavelength) of the light represents a *red shift* or a shift toward the red region of the spectrum. In other words, a light source (star) moving away from us is recognized by a shift toward the red region (lower frequency and longer wavelength) of the spectrum. If the light source is moving toward us, it is recognized by a shift toward the blue region (higher frequency and shorter wavelength) of the spectrum.

The Doppler Effect is similar to an everyday occurrence that we experience when a train is moving toward us or away from us. When a train is moving toward us, the pitch or frequency of its whistle sound increases. And when the train is moving away from us, the pitch or frequency of its whistle sound decreases.

Note to the reader: The following two topics are the major conceptual and experimental breakthroughs that led from classical Newtonian physics to Einstein's special theory of relativity.

Maxwell's Equations of Electromagnetism

In 1864, James Clerk Maxwell (1831–1879), Scottish born physicist, discovered four equations or laws of electromagnetism. These equations were considered to be "the most momentous mathematical discovery in the history of electrical science." Based on these equations, Maxwell postulated how electromagnetic waves are generated and propagated. He also proposed that light was a form of electromagnetic radiation and using these equations, he was able to calculate the velocity of light which was found to be in perfect agreement with the measured velocity of 186,284 miles/second or one billion feet per second.

On the basis of Maxwell's discovery, Heinrich Hertz succeeded in generating, transmitting, and detecting electromagnetic waves (radio waves) in the laboratory. This is how radio communications began.

The Michelson and Morley Experiment— Physics at the Crossroads

Classical or Newtonian physics required the presence of a medium for the transmission of waves. For example, air is the medium for the transmission of sound waves, and water is the medium for the transmission of water waves. So it was assumed that the transmission of electromagnetic waves should require a medium. This hypothetical medium was called "ether." In 1887 A.A. Michelson and E.W. Morley, two American physicists, performed a landmark experiment to unequivocally determine the existence or nonexistence of an "ether." Using an extremely accurate and precise interferometer that could detect changes in the velocity of light as small as a fraction of a mile per second, they detected no change in the velocity of light when the earth was moving to or away from a light source. This experiment conclusively ruled out the existence of an "ether." The Michelson-Morley experiment presented physicists with a dilemma. Either an "ether" existed or the earth did not move. The "ether" concept, at that time, was required to explain electricity, magnetism and light. But the concept of an earth in motion was the bedrock of the cosmology of Copernicus, Galileo and Newton. This was the state of physics at the end of the nineteenth century that would require the genius of an Albert Einstein and his special theory of relativity.

Albert Einstein— The Greatest Intellect of the Twentieth Century

In 1905 Albert Einstein (1879–1955), American-German born physicist, provided physics with a solution to the "ether dilemma." He told physicists to forget about the "ether." Einstein then went on to propose his special theory of relativity, which can be summarized in the following two postulates: (1) The laws of physics are the same for all observers in uniform (straight-line unaccelerated) motion. (2) The speed of light is constant and is independent of the speed of its source.

Once one accepts the first postulate that the laws of physics are the same for all observers in uniform motion, and the second postulate that the velocity of light is constant and is independent of the velocity of its source, then it logically follows that all observers who are in uniform motion, irrespective of their individual velocities, should obtain the same measurement for the velocity of light.

This means that an observer traveling at 600 miles per hour, in uniform motion, and a second observer traveling at 2,000 miles per hour, in uniform motion, and a third observer traveling at 25,000 miles per hour, in uniform motion, would all obtain the same measurement for the velocity of light. (See Figure 6.2.)

In his interesting book, *Genesis and the Big Bang*, Dr. Schroeder provides a very clear explanation of Einstein's special theory of relativity:

> The special theory of relativity is based on two facts: the principle of relativity and the constant speed of light. The principle of relativity postulated by Galileo Galilei three hundred years ago, was updated by Einstein. It states that all the laws of physics (which are really no more than the laws of nature) are the same in all unaccelerated systems: those systems having smooth, uniform motion. Such systems, in the jargon of physics, are called *inertial reference frames.*
>
> A reference frame is how you see yourself in relation to the world. At times, it is not inertial, such as when you are rocking in a rocking chair looking at a stationary object. The principle of relativity tells us that as long as we are within an inertial reference frame we cannot use the laws of physics to determine the frame's motion because that motion has no effect on any of the dimensions that we measure within the frame. This is why there is no sensation of motion while flying at a constant speed in calm weather. On the other hand, the constantly changing motion of the rocking chair makes our system noninertial and so we can feel our movement.[1]

Einstein's special theory of relativity also included the following postulates: (3) Energy and mass are equivalent ($E=mc^2$), and (4) the velocity of light is constant and nothing that has mass can travel faster than light.

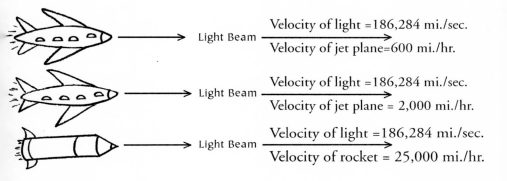

Figure 6.2. An illustration showing that the velocity of light is independent of the velocity of a light source in uniform motion.

In 1915, Einstein proposed his general theory of relativity. In this theory he described the universe as a space-time continuum with gravity being a property of the geometry of space. In Newton's universe, gravity was the attractive force responsible for the moon's circling the earth in an elliptical orbit, the planets' circling the sun in elliptical orbits, and the movements of all the heavenly bodies. Einstein's model of the universe could describe the movements of the heavenly bodies with greater accuracy than Newton's law of universal gravitation. In addition, Einstein's general theory of relativity suggested an expanding universe. However, Einstein, like Newton, firmly believed in a static universe. Because of this, he introduced into his theory a cosmological constant to cancel out the expansion of the universe that his theory required. In later years, he would confess that this was the greatest mistake that he made in his life. In evaluating Einstein's general theory of relativity, it should be noted that all of the predictions made by his theory have been confirmed to date by calculation, observation, and experimentation.

For example, Einstein's prediction that gravity would bend light was conclusively confirmed May 29,1919, by the famous English Astronomer, Sir Arthur Stanley Eddington. In his book, *Stephen Hawking's Universe; The Cosmos Explained,* Stephen Hawking provides us with the following interesting and informative details of this experiment:

> Just after the First World War, the British astronomer, Arthur Stanley Eddington led a team which aimed to see if the mass of the sun could deflect the light from a star as the sun passed between the star and the Earth. Naturally, the sun's light would be far too bright for us to see the star when this happened, except in one special circumstance: during a total eclipse. So Eddington and his team carefully worked out the "normal" position of a particular star in relation to its neighbors in the night sky, having determined that the sun would be directly between this star and the Earth at the time of a total eclipse of the sun in the year 1919. The plan was to photograph the area around the sun at the time of the eclipse, when the moon was blocking out all the sun's light. All the stars would thus be revealed in their usual positions; except, of course, for the star being studied.
>
> If Einstein was right, the mass of the sun would have had a gravitational effect on the light from the star, bending it so that the star would appear in a different position from normal. In fact, if Einstein was completely right, it would appear to be in the precise position predicted by Einstein's equations. And, sure enough, when the eclipse came, that was exactly where the star appeared to be.
>
> Eddington's experiment was important because it proved that Einstein's theory of gravity (rather than Newton's) was correct. More specifically, it showed that light was indeed bent, as it traveled through space, by anything with mass which crossed its path.[2]

It is said that when Einstein was informed of the existence of a book titled, *100 Authors Against Einstein,* he responded, "Why one hundred? If I were wrong, one would have been enough."[3] It is reported that when Einstein was offered the presidency of the new state of Israel that his response was, "Politics is for the moment, but an equation is for eternity."

Edwin Hubble—
The Man Who Took Us to the Edge of the Universe

It was in 1929 that man's optical journey to the outer limits of the universe was realized. In that year Edwin Hubble (Edwin Powell Hubble, 1889–1953, American astronomer) discovered that the universe was indeed expanding. By means of the 100-inch telescope on Mt. Wilson, he and his associates were able to see distant galaxies at the edge of the universe and to determine by means of the red shift that these galaxies were racing away from us and from each other. By means of the Doppler principle, they found that the farther away a galaxy, the faster it was moving (Hubble's law). Thus, they were forced to conclude that the universe was indeed expanding.

It should be noted that in 1922, seven years before Hubble's discovery of an expanding universe, the Russian physicist and mathematician, Alexander Friedman, embraced Einstein's general theory of relativity along with its requirement of a non static (expanding) universe. [4]

Georges Henri Lemaitre (1894–1966), Belgian astrophysicist, a mathematician-priest and a member of the faculty of the pontifical academy of the Vatican, had previously pointed out to Einstein that his (Einstein's) theory of relativity does allow for an expansion of the universe. At first, Einstein rejected Lemaitre's arguments and told him that his physics was not too good. However, after Hubble's discovery of an expanding universe, Einstein visited Hubble in 1951 and was later joined by Lemaitre. It is reported that at this meeting Lemaitre continued to argue that the theory of relativity does allow for an expanding universe. Lemaitre's argument backed by Hubble's observation of an expanding universe was overwhelming. It is said that Einstein rose from the table and said, "This is the most beautiful thing I've ever seen." Then he acknowledged that his introduction of a cosmological constant was the greatest blunder that he had ever made.

The Bible and the Concept of an Expanding Universe

For three hundred years the belief in a static universe prevailed in spite of the fact that both science and revelation support the concept of an expanding universe. A static universe was known to be inconsistent with Newton's law of universal gravitation, and there are several statements in the Bible that suggest the concept of an expanding universe. The following are some of these statements:

> He hath made the earth by his power, he hath established the world by his wisdom, and hath stretched out the heavens by his discretion.
>
> —Jer. 10:12

> He hath made the earth by his power, he hath established the world by his wisdom, and hath stretched out the heavens by his understanding.
>
> —Jer. 51:15

> Thus saith God the Lord, he that created the heavens, and stretched them out.
>
> —Isa. 42:5

> I have made the earth, and created man upon it: I, *even* my hands, have stretched out the heavens, and all their hosts have I commanded.
>
> —Isa. 45:12

> Mine hand also hath laid the foundation of the earth, and my right hand hath spread the heavens: when I call unto them they stand up together.
>
> —Isa. 48:13

> Who coverest thyself with light as with a garment: who stretchest out the heavens like a curtain.
>
> —Ps. 104:2

> Which alone spreadeth out the heavens....
>
> —Job 9:8

> It is he that sitteth on the circle of the earth...that stretcheth out the heavens as a curtain, and spreadeth them out as a tent to dwell in.
>
> —Isa. 40:22

The Big Bang—The Moment of Creation

Hubble's discovery in 1929 of an expanding universe had profound cosmological significance. From an expanding universe, it is possible to extrapolate backward in time to "zero time" (the moment of the big bang) when the universe was infinitesimally small and had infinite density. Under these conditions all of the laws and theories of science would break down. Mathematicians refer to this condition as a singularity. In cosmology, a singularity is "a point at which space and time are infinitely distorted by gravitational forces...." Dr. Gerald Schroeder, in his book, *Genesis and the Big Bang*, provides us with an interesting theoretical picture of the moment of creation immediately following time zero:

> While the conditions that existed prior to the appearance of energy and matter are not known, we can attempt to describe them at the briefest instant following the beginning, at about 10^{-43} seconds after the start.... The temperature was 10^{32}K (100 million million million million million degrees Kelvin). For comparison, the temperature at the center of the Sun is about 15 million degrees Kelvin. The surface of the Sun is a mere 5,800K.

> Physics and mathematics, as we know them today, cannot deal with times earlier than 10^{-43} seconds after the beginning. Prior to that time, the temperatures and densities of matter exceeded those that can be described by the laws of nature as we now understand them. Because of this, cosmological theory cannot handle the actual time zero beginning of the universe in terms that relate to dimensions experienced by humans.

> As the study of events following the big bang is extended mathematically to earlier times, the size of the universe shrinks toward zero and, inversely, the temperature and density increase toward infinity. The actual instant of the beginning envisions, for physicists, a moment when an infinitely small point of space was packed with matter squeezed to an infinitely high density. This condition of infinities is referred to as a singularity, and singularities cannot be treated by conventional mathematics."[5]

In 1970 Roger Penrose and Stephen Hawking, two brilliant British mathematical physicists, developed a mathematical proof for the occurrence of a big bang.

Fred Hoyle—A Skeptic Becomes a Believer

The idea that the universe began with a big bang from a primeval primordial atom was not universally accepted by the scientific world. One of the leading opponents of the big bang theory was Fred Hoyle, a British mathematician at Cambridge University. It was Hoyle who derisively coined the expression, "big bang."

To counter the big bang theory, he and his associates spearheaded another school of thought known as the steady state theory. They argued that the universe need not to have begun with a big bang, but as the universe expanded, new matter was created. However, the steady state theory could not explain how the ninety-two chemical elements that make up the universe were originally formed. Supporters of the big bang theory argued that all these elements were formed at one time in the throes of a big bang.

The steady state theorists were on the defensive. They had to come up with a valid explanation for the synthesis of the elements. In the thermal nuclear reactions that take place in the stars, they found that the chemical elements up to and including iron (Atomic weight=56) were being synthesized. But no elements with atomic weights greater than iron were being formed. They still had to come up with an explanation for the synthesis of the elements heavier than iron.

The answer to their problem was discovered in analyzing the light emitted from a super nova. In a star there is a constant tension between the gravitational forces favoring contraction and the thermal nuclear forces favoring expansion. When the amount of hydrogen becomes inadequate to support the fusion process, the gravitational forces predominate and if the star is a massive one, it collapses upon itself in an enormous cataclysmic event, known as a super nova. It is estimated that in just a few seconds a super nova generates more energy than the sun will in its lifetime. Analysis of the light emitted by the super nova showed the "fingerprints" and "signatures" of the chemical elements heavier than iron. Thus, the supporters of the steady state school were able to explain the origin of the ninety-two chemical elements. However, they had no valid explanation for the origin of the humongous quantities of hydrogen and helium present in the universe and needed for fuel for the stars. Reluctantly, they conceded that the big bang was the only logical explanation for the source of these quantities of hydrogen and helium.

Bob Wilson—Discoverer of the "After Glow" of a Big Bang

In 1948, George Gamow, a student of Alexander Friedman, proposed that residual microwave radiation from the extremely hot initial state of the universe should still be present today. Fred Hoyle also suggested that if there had been a big bang, there should still be some residual or "fossil radiation" or heat remaining from such an event. In 1964, Bob Dickey and his associates at Princeton University began work on a project to detect this residual microwave radiation or the "after glow" of a big bang. However, two scientists, Bob Wilson and Arnold Penzias of the Bell Telephone Laboratories in New Jersey were using a similar device (a very sensitive microwave detector) to receive satellite radio transmission. In the spring of 1965, Wilson and Penzias accidentally discovered the residual microwave radiation (heat) left over from the "monstrous explosion" of a big bang. For this remarkable achievement, they were awarded in 1978 one of the highest accolades in science—the Nobel Prize in Physics.

George Smoot—
Glimpses of the Universe at the Moment of Creation

Big bang cosmologists believed that in the early period of the universe, there should have been regions having variations or irregularities in temperature and density to favor the coalescence of matter into stars and galaxies. They also believed that if these variations could be detected, they would not only provide additional evidence for the big bang theory, but would also provide a picture of the early universe shortly after its creation. Using a NASA satellite and instrumentation comparable to that used by Penzias and Wilson, George Smoot, a young cosmologist in California, succeeded in mapping the variations or irregularities in the residual microwave radiation that originated from a big bang. The picture that emerged was one showing the formation of galaxies in the cooler regions of the universe. This was indeed a reconstructed picture of the universe shortly after the moment of creation.

The Anthropic Principle—Overwhelming Evidence

In the fall of 1973, at an international scientific meeting celebrating the five hundredth anniversary of the birth of Nicolaus Copernicus, Brandon Carter, a cosmologist from Cambridge University and a colleague of Stephen Hawking, presented a paper that would forever demolish the concept of a random universe which came into existence without the intervention of a Creator-God. The title of his paper was "Large Number Coincidences and the Anthropic Principle in Cosmology." According to the anthropic (*anthropos*, Greek: "man") principle, all of the physical constants and other parameters of the universe appear to have been carefully, accurately, and precisely chosen or designed to make possible the existence of human life on planet Earth. Indeed, the universe seems to have been made for man and not man for the universe.

In his excellent book, *God The Evidence*, Patrick Glynn presents the following litany of some of the coincidences presented by Brandon Carter:

Even the most minor tinkering with the value of the fundamental forces of physics-gravity, electromagnetism, the nuclear strong force, or the nuclear weak force would have resulted in an unrecognizable universe: a universe consisting entirely of helium, a universe without protons or atoms, a universe without stars, or a universe that collapsed back in upon itself before the first moments of its existence were up. Changing the precise ratios of the masses of subatomic particles in relation to one another would have similar effects. Even such basics of life as carbon and water depend upon uncanny "fine-tuning" at the subatomic level, strange coincidences in values for which physicists had no other explanation. To take just a few examples:

1. Gravity is roughly 10^{39} times weaker than electromagnetism. If gravity had been 10^{33} times weaker than electromagnetism, "stars would be a billion times less massive and would burn a million times faster."

2. The nuclear weak force is 10^{28} times the strength of gravity. Had the weak force been slightly weaker, all the hydrogen in the universe would have been turned to helium (making water impossible, for example).

3. A stronger nuclear strong force (by as little as 2 percent) would have prevented the formation of protons—yielding a universe without atoms. Decreasing it by 5 percent would have given us a universe without stars.

4. If the difference in mass between a proton and a neutron were not exactly as it is—roughly twice the mass of an electron—then all neutrons would have become protons or vice versa. Say goodbye to chemistry as we know it—and to life.

5. The synthesis of carbon—the vital core of all organic molecules—on a significant scale involves what scientists view as an "astonishing" coincidence in the ratio of the strong force to electromagnetism. This ratio makes it possible for carbon-12 to reach an excited state of exactly 7.65 MeV at the temperature typical of the center of stars, which creates a resonance involving helium-4, beryllium-8, and carbon-12—allowing the necessary binding to take place during a tiny window of opportunity 10^{-17} seconds long.[6]

Finally, remarks about how weakening the nuclear strong force would affect, e.g., protons—they could no longer be persuaded to come together in atomic nuclei, so hydrogen would be the only element—can be re-expressed as arguments for the disastrousness of electromagnetism's becoming slightly more powerful."[7]

For a comprehensive listing of these coincidences, the reader is referred to John Leslie's excellent and informative book, *Universes.*

Thus, we see that the anthropic principle, based on the strange coincidences listed above, speaks convincingly and eloquently of a universe created with an incredible degree of order, precision and design in its structure.

Listen to what some famous scientists have said about the big bang and the anthropic principle:

Fred Hoyle

"The big bang theory requires a recent origin of the universe that openly invites the concept of creation."[8]

"A common sense interpretation of the facts suggests that a super-intellect has monkeyed with physics, as well as with chemistry and biology, and that there are no blind forces worth speaking about in nature. The numbers one calculates from the facts seem to me so overwhelming as to put this conclusion almost beyond question."[9]

Barry Parker

"If we accept the big bang theory, and most cosmologists now do, then a 'creation' of some sort is forced upon us."[8]

George Smoot

"There is no doubt that a parallel exists between the big bang as an event and the Christian notion of creation from nothing."[8]

Robert Jastrow

"For the scientist who has lived by his faith in the power of reason, the story ends like a bad dream. He has scaled the mountains of ignorance; he is about to conquer the highest peak; as he pulls himself over the final rock, *he is greeted by a band of theologians who have been sitting there for centuries* [emphasis added]."[9]

In conclusion, let us consider the words of Pope John Paul II in his address before the international conference on scientific cosmology in 1981. The conference was sponsored by the Vatican:

> Any scientific hypothesis on the origin of the world, such as that of a primeval atom from which the whole of the physical world derived, leaves open the problem concerning the beginning of the universe. Science cannot by itself resolve such a question: what is needed is that human knowledge that rises above physics and astrophysics and which is called metaphysics; it needs above all the knowledge that comes from the revelation of God.[10]

1   Gerald L. Schroeder, Ph.D., *Genesis and the Big Bang*, New York: Bantum Books, 1992, p. 41.

2   Stephen Hawking, *Stephen Hawking's Universe*, New York: Harper Collins Publishers, Inc., 1997, p. 165.

3   Stephen Hawking, *The Universe in a Nutshell*, New York: Banton, 2002, p. 26.

4   Stephen Hawking, *A brief History of Time: From the Big Bang to Black Holes*, New York: Bantam, 1990, p. 40.

5   Gerald L. Schroeder, Ph.D., *Genesis and the Big Bang*, New York, New York: Bantam Doubleday Dell Publishing Group, Inc., 1990, pp. 65, 66.

6 Patrick Glynn, *God The Evidence*, California: Prima Pub., 1997, p. 29–30.
7 John Leslie, *Universes*, London, Routledge, p. 38.
8 Erwin W. Lutzer, *Seven Reasons Why You Can Trust The Bible*, Chicago: Moody Press, 1998, p. 139.
9 Ibid., p. 151.
10 Patrick Glynn, *God The Evidence*, California, Prima Pub., 1997, p. 41.

CHAPTER SEVEN

The Age of the Earth, the Noachian Flood, and the Ice Age

Part 1: The Age of the Earth

In Chapter 5, it was stated that at the moment of creation, "in the beginning," an eternal, transcendent, omnipotent, omniscient, Creator-God created energy, matter, and the dimensions of space and time when He created the universe.

Genesis 1:1 tells us that, "In the beginning God created the heaven and the earth." This text refers to the creation of the universe including the starry heaven and terrestrial matter. At the moment of creation all of the cosmic matter (the 92 chemical elements) that would become the components of galaxies, stars, and planets came into existence by fiat creation (by command) and creation ex nihilo (out of nothing).

The "heaven" mentioned in Genesis 1:1 must refer to the starry heaven since the atmospheric heaven (the firmament) was not created until the second day of creation week. This would also explain why, according to science, the ages of stars approximate the age of the universe. The anthropic principle (see Chapter 6) also supports the idea that all of the matter in the universe was created at the same time.

Estimation of the Age of Planet Earth

For centuries, scientists have endeavored to measure (estimate) the age of Planet Earth. The two principal methods used are: (1) measurement of the salinity of the ocean, and (2) radiometric dating of rocks.

The ocean salinity method. The amount of salt carried by the rivers to the ocean each year has been estimated to be about 500 million (5.0×10^8) tons. The total amount of salt in the ocean has been estimated to be 50×10^{15} or 50 quadrillion tons. By dividing the present amount of salt in the ocean by the amount of salt carried to the ocean each year they obtain a figure of 100 million years. Assuming that the amount of salt carried to the ocean was much less during the early history of the earth scientists estimate the age of the earth to be one or more billion years.

Radiometric dating of rocks. Uranium-238 is known to decay through a series of intermediates to an end product known as lead-206 or radiogenic lead. By measuring the uranium-lead ratio in a rock one can estimate the age of a rock. Most studies based on this method lead to an age of about 2 billion years. Based on other studies, the age of planet earth has been estimated to be about 4.3 billion years.

Some Definitions

Before proceeding with a discussion of the age of the earth, it is helpful to define the following philosophical positions:

1. A *conservative creationist* believes that God created a universe which is relatively young (6,000–10,000 years).
2. A *liberal creationist* believes that God created the material of the earth "in the beginning" when He created the universe and that the universe is several billion years old.
3. A *theistic evolutionist* believes that God created the universe and then left it to evolve according to the laws of physics.
4. An *atheistic evolutionist* believes that the universe came into existence without the intervention of God and has evolved to its present state according to the laws of physics.

Table 7.1 Age of the Earth Based on Bible Chronology.[1]

Time Period	Septuagint	Masoretic	Samaritan
Years from the flood to AD 1975	4279	5158	4868
Age of the pre-flood world	1656	2262	1307
Time Noah was in the ark	1	1	1
Total time from creation week to AD 1975	5936	7421	6176

Table 7.1 age of the world tabulation based on 966 BC for the beginning of construction of Solomon's Temple. The numbers presented are to be taken as only approximate representations of the designated time periods.

From the philosophical positions and definitions stated above, it is evident that there is a diversity of opinion among believers in a Creator-God concerning the age of the earth and the universe. This diversity of opinion is due primarily to differences in interpretation rather than to deliberate contradictions of basic truths.

There are two major schools of thought concerning the age of the earth. These are: (1) the young earth theory and (2) the ancient earth theory.

The Young Earth Theory. According to this theory, the earth is not more than about 6,000 to 10,000 years old. Those who embrace this theory base their position on biblical chronology. Those who oppose this theory cite the following scientific evidence:

1. The amount of time required for light to travel from distant galaxies to the earth is consistent with a universe that is billions rather than thousands of years old.

2. Evidence from the radiometric dating of minerals suggests that the age of the earth is several orders of magnitude greater than 10,000 years.
3. Those creationists who support the young universe theory usually neglect to allow time for such events as the creation and existence of other worlds, the creation of angels, the creation of the sons of God, and the fall of Lucifer prior to creation week for this earth.

The Ancient Earth Theory. Big bang cosmology suggests that the universe was created about 15 billion years ago. Creationists who support the big bang theory believe that at the moment of creation, "in the beginning," an eternal, transcendent, omnipotent, omniscient Creator-God created energy, matter, and the dimensions of space and time when He created the universe. They also believe that at this time terrestrial matter was brought into existence. The arguments listed above against the young earth theory are also used to support the ancient earth theory. Those who oppose the ancient earth theory argue that God could have created the earth and the universe to appear much older than it actually is. But others argue that such a creation would be inconsistent with the perfect character of God. According to Dr. Mart de Groot, an astronomer and director at the Armagh Observatory in Northern Ireland, "To argue that God created these luminaries with their radiations filling the universe right from the beginning seems a bit contrived."[2] This also would be uncharacteristic of a God that cannot lie (Titus 1:2).

Biblical Genealogy and Chronology

Biblical chronology probably began in 1654 when James Ussher, the Archbishop of Ireland, announced to the world that creation began "at 9 o'clock a.m. on the twenty-sixth of October in the year 4004 BC." Ussher's pronouncement was based on biblical genealogies. He incorrectly assumed that there were no gaps in the biblical genealogies listed in the Bible. Today, theologians tell us that the genealogy lists in the Bible do not include every descendant. In some cases only the more important ancestors are listed. In addition, they indicate that the term "son" in genealogy often refers to a "descendant." This term "son" may refer to a son, a grandson, a great grandson, or someone farther down the line. It is for this reason that most of today's Christian scholars usually assume that creation week occurred about six to ten thousand years ago.

The Ages of Fossils

Those evolutionists who believe that life on planet earth can be measured in millions of years base their position on the age of minerals associated with fossils. They make the unsupported assumption that the age of the fossil is the same as the age of the mineral. Dr. Robert H. Brown of the Geoscience Research Institute demolishes this position by pointing out the error that evolutionists make when they assume that the age of the fossil is identical to the age of the mineral associated with it:

> The second area of evidence that should be mentioned here is the radiometric data concerning inorganic minerals associated with fossils. It has been commonly assumed that the radiometric "clocks" in these minerals were "set zero" when the mineral was brought into association with a fossil. This assumption is overly simplistic. It has not been scrutinized as it should have been, because it provides ages for fossils that appear to give support for the evolutionary viewpoint that became popular decades before radiometric-dating techniques were developed.[3]

Geological Eras

Evolutionists recognize the following six geological eras: Azoic, Archeozoic, Proterozoic, Paleozoic, Mesozoic and Cenozoic.

The Earth Structure and Changes

In terms of structure, our planet, earth, consists of the following four spheres: centrosphere, lithosphere, hydrosphere, and atmosphere.

The atmosphere is the envelope of gases surrounding the earth. It extends up to an altitude of about seventy miles. The hydrosphere consists of oceans, seas, lakes, and rivers on the surface of the earth. The lithosphere represents the rocky surface of the earth (the earth's crust). The centrosphere consists of two parts: the mantle and the core. The mantle can be further subdivided into the asthenosphere and the mesosphere. The asthenosphere is a thin, semi-plastic layer near the surface of the mantle. Below the asthenoshpere lies the mesosphere, which is a solid, dense layer. Seismic data suggests that the core consists of a solid inner core surrounded by a liquid under tremendously high pressure. From the surface of the earth to the surface of the core is approximately 1,800 miles, and from the surface of the core to the center of the earth is approximately 2,200 miles.

Diastrophism. Diastrophism refers to the structural changes that are taking place in the lithosphere. The lithosphere consists of continental and oceanic plates that float and move on the upper mantle like giant ice sheets on an ocean. The theory of plate tectonics describes the movement of these continental plates and the resultant formation of mountain building and occurrence of earthquakes and volcanoes.

Uniformitarianism. In geology, uniformitarianism is the teaching that the present structure of the lithosphere (crust of the earth) can be explained in terms of processes occurring at the present time. Uniformitarians believe that in the past there have been uniform, consistent and gradual changes in the structure of the crust of the earth. However, discoveries during the past twenty years have caused some scientists to question the validity of this theory. In his book, *It Couldn't Just Happen,* Dr. Lawrence O. Richards vividly describes an event that was a death knell to the theory of uniformitarianism:

> One day almost 3,400 years ago, in the Aegean Sea between Greece and Turkey, a 4,900-foot mountain shook. Then it exploded with the force of hundreds of hydrogen bombs. Hot volcanic fires shot miles into the sky, causing a fiery rain that spread out for miles, dropping ash one hundred feet thick on nearby islands.

> Then the rest of the island of Santorini dropped into a deep hole in the sea, causing tidal waves hundreds of feet high, rushing outward at two hundred miles an hour. Those waves smashed again and again into Crete, the nearby island center of a great civilization, and into other shores. Hundreds of thousands of people were killed, and the Minoan civilization was wiped out.

...Today we can still see the results of the eruption, marked on the surface of our Earth. We can dig through the volcanic ash that buried the nearby islands and filled the valleys of Crete, seventy miles away. We can measure the hole in the sea that the volcano blasted out 1,300 feet deep. And we can see the huge building stones on Crete that were torn from ancient palaces and tossed about like match sticks.

...The explosion of Santorini was a great catastrophe. Its recent discovery is just one of many discoveries made in the last twenty years that have affected the science of geology, which deals with the study of the Earth and its past.

For decades geologists accepted a teaching called "uniformitarianism." This is the belief that what we find in Earth's rocks and on its surface can be fully explained by processes taking place now. Uniformitarian geologists rejected the idea that Earth ever experienced any great catastrophes, such as the Flood described in Genesis. They argued that natural processes could account for everything, given enough time."[4]

The apostle Peter might have had uniformitarians in mind when he wrote, "Knowing this first, that there shall come in the last days scoffers, walking after their own lusts, And saying, Where is the promise of His coming? For since the fathers fell asleep, all things continue as *they were* from the beginning of creation" (2 Peter 3:3–4).

Catastrophism. Catastrophism is the belief that there have been major, geological catastrophes in the past history of the earth. Those who support this idea cite the Noachian Flood, and of course, the explosion of Mt. Santorini (C.1400 BC) described above.

Theory of Plate Tectonics. Early observations of the shapes of the continents suggested a complementarity between the shape of Africa and South America and Europe and North America. Based on these observations Antonio Snider made a sketch of Africa and South America fitting together as one land mass. In 1912, the German meteorologist Alfred Wegener theorized that Africa and South America were originally one landmass, which he called "Pangea" which means "all lands." He further suggested that the present separation of these two continents was due to a division of the earth at some time in the past. It is interesting to note that the books of Genesis and 1 Chronicles speak of the division of the earth after the Flood. "And unto Eber were born two sons: the name of one *was* Peleg; for in his days was the earth divided; and his brother's name *was* Joktan" (Gen. 10:25). "And unto Eber were born two sons: the name of the one *was* Peleg; because in his days was the earth divided: and his brother's name *was* Joktan" (1 Chron. 1:19).

Wegener supported his theory of continental drift with the observations that the fossils found on the Western Coast of Africa were quite similar to those found on the Eastern coast of South America, and fossils found in Europe matched those found on the shores of North America.

In the 1950s and 60s impressive evidence in support of the continental drift theory began to emerge. Some of this evidence came from (1) sonar mapping of the ocean floor, (2) paleomagnetism of rocks on the ocean floor, and (3) fossils lying on the ocean floor.

As a result of sonar mapping, the Mid-Atlantic Ridge was discovered. The Mid-Atlantic Ridge is part of a global mid-ocean ridge system that circles the earth. The discovery of the Mid-Atlantic Ridge and seafloor spreading eventually led to the development of Plate Tectonic theory. Tectonics refers to the deformation in the crust of the earth such as volcanoes, earthquakes and mountain building. The theory of Plate Tectonics seeks to explain these deformations in terms of the movements of continental plates. According to Plate Tectonic Theory, the lithosphere is made up of semirigid plates that move on the asthenosphere. Some of these plates consist of continents and ocean floors, while others consist only of ocean floors. There are approximately twelve tectonic plates on the surface of the earth. These are the North American, the Pacific, the European, the South American, the Australian, the African, the Indian, the China and other plates. The North American Plate extends from the mid-Atlantic Ridge all the way to the San Andreas Fault. People living in San Diego, San Francisco and Hawaii live on the Pacific Plate. The San Andreas Fault is a transform boundary between the North American Plate and the Pacific Plate. The tendency of the Pacific Plate to slide north with respect to the North American Plate is the reason for the occurrence of earthquakes along the San Andreas Fault. The movements of tectonic plates help to explain such geological phenomena as mountain building, earthquakes and volcanoes. These geological phenomena usually occur at the interface of two plates, which is known as a plate boundary. Three kinds of plate boundaries are known based on their relative movements:

Divergent boundaries occur when two plates move away from each other; convergent boundaries occur when two plates move towards each other; transform boundaries occur when plates slide by each other.

At the occurrence of a divergent boundary, magma from the mantle rises between the plates, is cooled and solidifies to form a ridge. An important divergent boundary is the mid-Atlantic Ridge, which runs south between Africa and South America, and north between North America and Eurasia.

Since the occurrence of a divergent boundary results in the formation of new crust, some other process must take place in order to reduce the amount of crust on the earth's surface. The process that does this is the formation of a subduction zone at a convergent boundary. At this boundary the crust of one plate is subducted below the surface of the adjacent plate. A transform boundary occurs where two plates interact by sliding by each other.

The following are the principal evidences in support of plate tectonic theory:

The complementarity of the shapes of the continents (North America and Europe, South America and Africa). The similarity of rocks, minerals, and fossils on opposite sides of the North Atlantic and the South Atlantic (e.g. fossils in Wales match those in New England, and diamond fields in Africa match those in Brazil). The distribution of volcanoes and earthquakes, especially those located in the "ring of fire" along the Pacific Ocean. The discovery of ocean-floor spreading and the study of ocean floor topography, especially the formation of the Mid-Atlantic Ridge. The discovery of a linear relationship between the ages of volcanic islands and their distances from the Mid-Atlantic Ridge (e.g. Iceland, the Azores and the Falkland Islands). The study of the paleomagnetism of the ocean floor.

In summary, Wegener's theory of continental drift led to the discovery of seafloor spreading, which led to plate tectonic theory, which helps to explain the formation of new crust and the disappearance of old crusts on the surface of the earth along with such geological phenomena as earthquakes, volcanoes and mountain building.

Part 2: The Noachian Flood

The creation story, the Noachian Flood, and the resurrection of Jesus Christ are probably the three teachings of the Bible which are most often attacked by skeptics, scoffers and unbelievers. In this section we shall present impressive evidence in support of the occurrence of a universal flood.

I. Biblical Evidences for the Flood

In view of the established credibility of the Bible (see pages 26–36 in Chapter 1), the evidence from the Bible in support of a universal flood should not and cannot be ignored. The following are some of these evidences.

In the book of Ezekiel, God speaks of Noah as a real person. "Though these three men, Noah, Daniel, and Job, were in it, they should deliver *but* their own souls by their righteousness, saith the Lord GOD" (Ezek. 14:14). Jesus, in His teachings, also referred to Noah as a real person and to the Flood. "But as the days of Noe *were*, so shall also the coming of the Son of man be. For as in the days that were before the flood they were eating and drinking, marrying and giving in marriage, until the day that Noe entered into the ark, And knew not until the flood came, and took them all away; so shall also the coming of the Son of man be" (Matt. 24:37–39).

The writer of Hebrews also makes reference to Noah and his ark. "By faith Noah, being warned of God of things not seen as yet, moved with fear, prepared an ark to the saving of his house; by the which he condemned the world, and became heir of the righteousness which is by faith" (Heb. 11:7). Likewise, the apostle Peter mentions the Flood several times in his epistles.

> Knowing this first, that there shall come in the last days scoffers, walking after their own lusts, And saying, Where is the promise of his coming? For since the fathers fell asleep, all things continue as

they were from the beginning of the creation. For this they willingly are ignorant of, that by the word of God the heavens were of old, and the earth standing out of the water and in the water: Whereby the world that then was, being overflowed with water, perished.

—2 Pet. 3:3–6

Which sometime were disobedient, when once the longsuffering of God waited in the days of Noah, while the ark was a-preparing, wherein few, that is, eight souls were saved by water.

—1 Pet. 3:20

And spared not the old world, but saved Noah the eighth *person,* a preacher of righteousness, bringing in the flood upon the world of the ungodly.

—2 Pet. 2:5

Speaking through the prophet Isaiah, God compares his faithfulness to the waters of Noah. "For this *is as* the waters of Noah unto me: for *as* I have sworn that the waters of Noah should no more go over the earth; so have I sworn that I would no more be wroth with thee, nor rebuke thee" (Isa. 54:9). The phenomenon of the rainbow is enduring evidence of the Flood. "I do set my bow in the cloud, and it shall be for a token of a covenant between me and the earth. And it shall come to pass, when I bring a cloud over the earth, that the bow shall be seen in the cloud: And I will remember my covenant, which is between me and you and every living creature of all flesh; and the waters shall no more become a flood to destroy all flesh" (Gen. 9:13–15).

The tower of Babel, which was being constructed as a means of escape from another flood, and the diversity of languages and races are evidences of the Flood. "And they said, Go to, let us build us a city and a tower, whose top *may reach* unto heaven…" (Gen. 11:4). "Therefore is the name of it called Babel; because the Lord did there confound the language of all the earth: and from thence did the Lord scatter them abroad upon the face of the earth" (Gen. 11:9). It is believed that as a result of the confounding of the languages of the builders of the tower of Babel and the subsequent scattering of the people on the basis of linguistic commonality, climatic and environmental forces along with inbreeding resulted in the diversity of races.

II. Topographical Evidence for a Flood

It is believed by many that the present topography of the earth can best be explained on the basis of a universal flood. For example, there are strong arguments in support of the idea that the Grand Canyon is a direct result of the Noachian Flood.

III. Fossil Evidences for the Flood

Lecturer Kent Hovind of Creation Science Evangelism reports that "the top 3,000 feet of Mt. Everest is made up of sedimentary rock packed with seashells and [fossils of] other ocean-dwelling animals...." Hovind also states that "bent rock layers, fossil graveyards, and poly-strata fossils are best explained by a Flood."[5]

IV. Evidence for the Flood Based on Flood Legends from Many Parts of the World

Lecturer Kent Hovind of Creation Science Evangelism reports, "There are more than 270 flood legends from all parts of the world. Most have many similarities to the Genesis story."[5]

In his book, *It Couldn't Just Happen*, Lawrence Richards reports the following:

One of many examples of fossil finds that do not fit the evolutionary theory is found in a great slab of sedimentary rock near Agate Springs, Nebraska. This slab holds the bones of some 9,000 different animals, all jumbled up together. These animals, which include rhinoceroses, camels, giant boars, and many other strange as well as modern animals, were all tossed together by some violent flood and were buried quickly, before their bodies could decay or be eaten. The sudden burial together of kinds of animals who should not be found in the same part of the world is the kind of find that cannot be accounted for by the Theory of Evolution."[6]

V. Irrefutable Evidence in Support of a Universal Flood

The fact that the Flood has been estimated to have occurred 4,400 years ago and that there are no living trees that are older that 4,400 years is irrefutable evidence in support of a worldwide Flood.

Those who contend that the Noachian Flood was local rather than universal fail to realize that a local Noachian flood is not consistent with God's covenant to Noah as stated in Genesis 9:11 and Isaiah 54:9. If God's covenant to Noah were based on a local flood, then the occurrence of any local or regional flood would be a violation of His covenant.

VI. Coal and Oil as Evidences of the Flood

(Please see Appendix B.)

In her book, *Principles of True Science,* the noted Bible commentator E.G. White states the following concerning the origin of coal and oil deposits in the earth:

> Before the Flood there were immense forests. The trees were many times larger than any trees which we now see. They were of great durability. They would know nothing of decay for hundreds of years. At the time of the Flood these forests were torn up or broken down and buried in the earth. In some places large quantities of these immense trees were thrown together and covered with stones and earth by the commotions of the flood. They have since petrified and become coal, which accounts for the large coal beds which are now found.... Coal and oil are generally to be found where there are no burning mountains or fiery issues."[7]

Biblical Facts about the Flood

The following are some of the important Biblical facts concerning the Flood.

1. Noah preached to the antediluvians for one hundred and twenty years before the Flood. "And the LORD said, My spirit shall not always strive with man, for that he also *is* flesh: yet his days shall be an hundred and twenty years" (Gen. 6:3).

2. Duration of the Flood:
    a. At the beginning of the Flood, it rained for forty days and forty nights. "And the rain was upon the earth forty days and forty nights" (Gen. 7:12).
    b. The waters prevailed for one hundred and fifty days. "And the waters prevailed upon the earth an hundred and fifty days" (Gen. 7:24).
    c. After one lunar year (360 days) and ten days the earth became dry again. "And it came to pass in the six hundredth and first year, in the first *month*, the first *day* of the month, the waters were dried up from off the earth…" (Gen. 8:13). "And in the second month, on the seven and twentieth day of the month, was the earth dried" (Gen. 8:14).
3. The waters came from below and above the earth. "…The same day were all the fountains of the great deep broken up, and the windows of heaven were opened" (Gen. 7:11).
4. The waters covered all of the mountains. "And the waters prevailed exceedingly upon the earth; and all the high hills, that *were* under the whole heaven, were covered. Fifteen cubits upward did the waters prevail; and the mountains were covered" (Gen. 7:19–20).
5. The Flood destroyed all living creatures, except for those that were in the ark and in the sea. "And every living substance was destroyed which was upon the face of the ground, both man, and cattle, and the creeping things, and the fowl of the heaven; and they were destroyed from the earth: and Noah only remained *alive*, and they that *were* with him in the ark" (Gen. 7:23).

Sources of the Flood Waters

Skeptics often ask the following questions: (1) What were the sources of water needed for a universal flood? (2) Is there enough water on planet earth to cover the entire surface of the earth, including the highest mountains?

The following Bible texts provide a clear picture of an earth that was covered with water in the beginning when it was created:

> For this they willingly are ignorant of, that by the word of God the heavens were of old, and the earth standing out of the water and in the water: Whereby the world that then was, being overflowed with water perished.
>
> —2 Pet. 3:5–6

> And the earth was without form, and void; and darkness *was* upon the face of the deep. And the spirit of God moved upon the face of the waters.
>
> —Gen. 1:2

> And God said, Let there be a firmament in the midst of the waters, and let it divide the waters from the waters. And God made the firmament, and divided the waters which *were* under the firmament from the waters which *were* above the firmament: and it was so.
>
> —Gen. 1:6–7

> In the sixth hundredth year of Noah's life, in the second month, the seventeenth day of the month, the same day were all the fountains of the great deep broken up, and the windows of heaven were opened.
>
> —Gen. 7:11

The above texts clearly indicate that in the pre-Flood earth, there was water under the crust of the earth, water above the crust of the earth (rivers and lakes), and water above the atmosphere. Even today, most of the surface of the earth is covered with water. It is estimated that the average depth of the oceans is two and a half miles. However, there are some extraordinary depths in the ocean. For example, Swire depth, near Japan, is 35,000 feet deep while Mt. Everest, the highest mountain on earth, is only 29,000 feet high. Thus we see that the greatest depth exceeds the highest height. Science tells us that if all of the mountains and hills were flattened, water would cover the entire earth.

Results of the Flood

The following are three major results of the flood which have had a profound effect on planet earth.

1. The Precipitous Decline in Longevity

The Bible reveals a precipitous decline in the life span of man after the Flood. For example, Noah lived for 950 years; his son Shem lived 600 years; Arphaxad lived 438 years; Salah lived 433 years; Eber lived 464 years; and Peleg, the fifth from Noah and also the first man to live fewer than 400 years, lived 239 years. It is reasonable to assume that at the time of the Flood there was a catastrophic change in the eco-system of the human race that led to this precipitous decline in longevity of man from 950 years to 239 years over a period of approximately 200 years. Nahmanides (Moses ben Nahman, CE 1194-1270, Spain, Israel; also known as Ramban), one of the earliest commentators on Genesis, claimed that "Prior to the flood, the conditions on the Earth favored long life. The upheaval that accompanied the Flood changed the atmosphere and climate causing a gradual shortening of individual life spans."[8]

The Bible commentator E.G. White provides us with another cause for the shortening of the life span of postdiluvian men: "God saw that the ways of man were corrupt, and that he was disposed to exalt himself proudly against his Creator, and to follow the inclinations of his own heart. And he permitted that long-lived race to eat animal food to shorten their sinful lives. Soon after the flood the race began to rapidly decrease in size, and in length of years."[9]

2. The Division of the Earth

It is also interesting to note that Genesis 10:25 and 1 Chronicles 1:19 make the significant statement that the earth was divided in the days of Peleg. "And unto Eber were born two sons: the name of one *was* Peleg; for in his days was the earth divided; and his brother's name *was* Joktan" (Gen. 10:25). "And unto Eber were born two sons: the name of the one *was* Peleg; for in his days was the earth divided; and his brother's name *was* Joktan" (1 Chron. 1:19).

3. The Tilting of the Earth on its Axis and the Resulting Changes in Climate

Genesis 8:22 is the first mention of cold weather in the Bible and suggests that there was a drastic change in the climate of the earth following the Flood. "While the earth remaineth, seedtime and harvest, and cold and heat, and summer and winter, and day and night shall not cease (Gen. 8:22).

Science tells us that the progression of the seasons, from fall to winter to spring and to summer, is due primarily to the tilting of the earth on its axis. In the northern hemisphere summer occurs when the axis of the earth is tilted towards the sun. This causes the rays of the sun to strike the surface of the northern hemisphere more directly, resulting in the absorption of maximum solar radiation (heat). This tilting of the earth also results in longer days (more heating) and shorter nights (less cooling) during the months of summer in the northern hemisphere. Winter occurs when the axis of the earth is tilted away from the sun, resulting in the rays of the sun striking the northern hemisphere obliquely and resulting in the absorption of less solar radiation (less heat). This tilting of the axis away from the sun also results in longer nights (more cooling) and shorter days (less heating) during the winter months in the northern hemisphere. During fall and spring the axis of the earth is tilted neither towards nor away from the sun, resulting in relatively mild temperatures.

In the northern hemisphere, summer begins on June 21, the date of the Summer Solstice. On this date, the sun rises in the east and travels over the Tropic of Cancer and sets in the west. "The Tropic of Cancer is the northernmost latitude reached by the overhead sun." This is also the day that the northern hemisphere has its longest day and shortest night.

In the northern hemisphere, winter begins on December 21, the date of the Winter Solstice. On this date, the sun rises in the east and travels over the Tropic of Capricorn and sets in the west. "The Tropic of Capricorn is the southernmost latitude reached by the overhead sun." This is also the day that the northern hemisphere has its longest night and shortest day.

In the northern hemisphere, fall begins on September 23, the date of the Autumnal Equinox. On this date the sun rises in the east, travels directly over the equator, and sets in the west. This is also the date when night and day are everywhere equal.

In the northern hemisphere, spring begins on March 21, the date of the Vernal Equinox. On this date the sun rises in the east, travels over the equator, and sets in the west. This is also the date when night and day are everywhere equal.

Thus we see that the progression of the seasons is due primarily to the tilting of the earth on its axis and the inclination of this axis either towards the sun or away from the sun as the earth revolves around the sun during the course of one year.

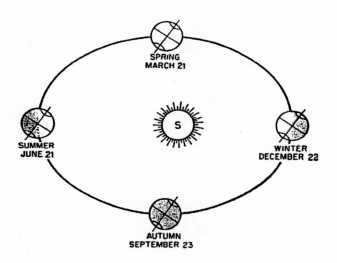

Figure 7.1. The positions of the axis of the earth during the solar year. (From McCorkle, "The Physical World," New York, The McGraw-Hill Book Company.)

4. The Phenomenon of Rain

The Bible implies that it did not rain before the Flood. Note Genesis 2:6: "But there went up a mist from the earth, and watered the whole face of the ground." Also the phenomenon of the rainbow did not occur until after the Flood. Note Genesis 9:13: "I do set my bow in the cloud, and it shall be for a token of a covenant between me and the earth."

Since it did not rain before the Flood, and since after the Flood rain became a normal occurrence, it is evident that the Flood created the conditions necessary for the formation of rain. Science tells us that when warm, moist air rises and is then cooled, that the air becomes saturated or supersaturated and the excess moisture condenses or precipitates in the form of rain. If the temperature at which precipitation occurs is 32°F or below, the precipitation will be in the form of snow. From this explanation we see that there are two prerequisites for rain formation. Warm, moist air must be present and a lifting mechanism must be available. This lifting mechanism may be an approaching cold front, a low-pressure area, or some other mechanism for producing convection (circulation). The following are some examples of rain formation:

1. Rain formation due to an approaching cold front: When a cold front (a cold mass of air) moves into a warm mass of air, the warm air rises, is cooled, and condensation in the form of rain occurs.
2. Rain formation due to a low pressure: A low pressure in the atmosphere is characterized by warm air rising. A high-pressure region in the atmosphere is characterized by air descending. Thus we see that a low pressure in the atmosphere is capable of producing the lift necessary for rain formation. In the tropics, rain occurs by the action of a variety of convection currents on warm, moist air.

From this understanding of rain formation, it is evident that the Flood produced an atmosphere characterized by cold masses of air, warm masses of air, and violent circulations (storms) when these different air masses collide. The evidences for the Flood and the results of the Flood discussed above represent powerful arguments and convincing evidence in support of a universal Flood.

The Sudden Extinction of the Dinosaurs

Proponents of the theory of evolution are at a loss to explain the sudden extinction of the dinosaurs and other mammoth reptiles. The dinosaur, which sometimes reached a length of eighty feet, and the ptero-dactyl, a flying reptile with a wing span of approximately thirty feet, along with other huge creatures, once roamed the surface of the earth and then suddenly and mysteriously became extinct. On the other hand, theistic creationists who believe in the credibility of the Bible have a simple an-swer for the disappearance of these large creatures: the Noachian Flood.

The following informative statements by the noted Bible commen-tator E.G. White give a clear understanding of the sudden disappear-ance of these large animals:

There were a class of very large animals which perished at the flood. God knew that the strength of man would decrease, and these mam-moth animals could not be controlled by feeble man.

Bones of men and animals are found in the earth, in mountains, and in valleys, showing that much larger men and beasts once lived upon the earth. I was shown that very large, powerful animals existed be-fore the Flood which do not now exist.

Every species of animal which God had created were preserved in the ark. The confused species, which God did not create, which were the result of amalgamation, were destroyed by the Flood.[10]

Another school of thought suggests that baby dinosaurs were in-cluded in the ark, but the drastic and adverse climatic conditions fol-lowing the flood did not favor their development into the mammoth creatures that existed before the flood.

Part 3: The Ice Age

The Bible is silent concerning the occurrence of an ice age, but the earth itself bears record of such an event. For example, it has been ob-served that, "much of the land areas in the northern part of the United

States and Europe are covered by a heterogeneous mass of boulders, rocks, and soil which are unlike the rock strata of the region.... The casual observer can discover many evidences of glaciation. One famous example is a boulder in Bronx Park in New York City which rests on a striated base of a different type of rock. Many rocks show parallel striations on the surface as a result of scratches due to rocks embedded in the moving glaciers."[11]

It is believed that "The Great Lakes and many modern rivers, such as the Illinois River, were formed at the time of the last glacial age. The great number of lakes in Minnesota and Wisconsin are of glacial origin. It is even possible in some cases to trace the shore line of older lakes and rivers which disappeared during glacial epochs and were superseded by other bodies of water."[11]

Just how the evidences of a universal Flood and the evidences of previous ice ages are related is not clear. One theory speculates that an icy comet from outer space entered our solar system, struck the earth, initiated the Flood, and produced massive amounts of ice and snow in the Arctic and Antarctic regions of the earth. However, this is mostly speculation. But the discoveries of many frozen, intact mammoth animals in the Arctic and Antarctic regions of the earth are not speculation. These are facts.

Concerning the ice age and periods of glaciation, it is prudent to recall Deuteronomy 29:29: "The secret *things belong* to the LORD our God: but those *things which* are revealed *belong* unto us and to our children for ever...."

---

1   Robert H. Brown, "How Old Is the World?", *Review and Herald*, Washington, D.C.: Review and Herald Publishing Association, 1975, p. 5.

2   Dr. Mart de Groot, "God and the Big Bang" *Adventist Review*, Hagerstown, MD.: *Adventist Review*, Aug. 13, 1992, vol. 169. p. 14.

3   Robert H. Brown, "How Old Is the World?," *Review and Herald,*
    Washington, D.C.: Review and Herald Publishing Association,
    1975, p. 8.
4   Lawrence O. Richards, *It Couldn't Just Happen,* Fort Worth, Tex.:
    Word, Inc, 1987, pp. 35–37.
5   Kent Hovind, *Creation Science Evangelism (Seminar Notebook),*
    Pensacola, Florida, 1999, p. 20.
6   Lawrence Richards, p. 89–90.
7   Ellen G. White, *Principles of True Science,* Payson, Arizona: Leaves
    of Autumn Books, Inc., reprinted 1986, p. 87.
8   Gerald L. Schroeder, Ph.D., *Genesis and the Big Bang,* New York,
    New York: Bantam Doubleday Dell Publishing Group, Inc., 1990,
    p. 32.
9   Ellen G. White, p. 31.
10 Ellen G. White, *Spiritual Gifts,* Vol. 4, Washington, D.C.: Review
    and Herald Publishing Association, 1945, p. 121.
11 Paul McCorkle, *The Physical World,* New York: McGraw-Hill Book
    Company, Inc., 1956, p. 107–108.

CHAPTER EIGHT

The Origin of Life on Planet Earth

Concerning the origin of life on planet earth, the Bible is unmistakably clear. In his speech on Mars' Hill, the apostle Paul refers to God not only as the Creator but also as the Lifegiver: "God that made the world and all things therein, seeing that he is Lord of heaven and earth, dwelleth not in temples made with hands; Neither is worshipped with men's hands, as though he needed any thing, seeing he giveth to all life, and breath, and all things" (Acts 17:24–25).

Genesis 1:11, 20–22 describes the beginning of life on the third and fifth days of creation week:

> And God said, Let the earth bring forth grass, the herb yielding seed, and the fruit tree yielding fruit after his kind, whose seed is in itself, upon the earth: and it was so.
>
> —Gen. 1:11

> And God said, Let the waters bring forth abundantly the moving creature that hath life, and the fowl that may fly above the earth in the open firmament of heaven. And God created great whales, and every living creature that moveth, which the waters brought forth abundantly, after their kind, and every winged fowl after his kind: and God saw that it was good.
>
> —Gen. 1:20–21

On the third and fifth days of creation week, we see the first appearance of plant and animal life on the earth. Both plant and animal life emanated from a Creator God. Whereas evolutionary theories postulate the origin of life from "spontaneous generation," creationists believe that life can come only from a life-giving God. Dr. Coffin's comment on life originating by spontaneous generation is quite informative:

> An untruth asserted often enough may, in time, be accepted no matter how wrong it is. This psychological experience, referred to as brainwashing, has happened to many people without their being aware of it. We have been told so often that life came from nonliving material that many now believe in it. ...Scientists such as Louis Pasteur later convinced the world by concrete scientific experimentation that spontaneous generation is not possible.[1]

Some evolutionists, who reject the concept of spontaneous generation, postulate that terrestrial life could have come from outer space. Creationists find this concept to be untenable and without merit. Commenting on this assumption, Dr. Hoen writes:

> So while believing in some form of spontaneous   generation, evolutionists in general at least deny the "fantastic speculation" that simple living creatures rode into this earth from some remote heavenly body. There is abundant reason for this denial, for the conditions of interplanetary space are not favorable for the maintenance of life, and the high temperatures of arriving meteors are still less favorable.[2]

Now, if terrestrial life did not originate from spontaneous generation or from outer space, the question remains: Where did life come from? The only reasonable, logical, and sensible answer is that life came from a life-giving Creator God. Those who believe in the evolutionary sequence from atoms to organic molecules to complex living organisms fail to realize the profound and vast difference between a complex organism and a living organism. At the moment of death, *biological complexity is still present but life is not.* No one has ever observed the process from inanimate to animate (from death to life), except observers of miraculous resurrections or restorations of life. But the opposite process from animate to inanimate (from life to death) is ubiquitously pervasive.

The statement that life can only come from a life source or that life can come only from pre-existing life is as much a law as is Newton's law of universal gravitation. In science a law is considered to be an "economy-of-thought" description of the way nature behaves. Thus, Newton's law of universal gravitation is a description of the way nature behaves. For thousands of years before Newton codified or articulated his law of universal gravitation, the consequence of Newton's law of universal gravitation was observed. It was noted without exception, that all bodies heavier than air and lacking a propulsion system of their own would fall to the earth. Likewise, for thousands of years up until the present time, it has been observed in nature, without exception, that *life comes only from a source of life* (life source). This statement is as valid a law as is Newton's law of universal gravitation.

The following is a list of some insurmountable barriers to the spontaneous generation of life:

The Problem of an Initial Pre-curser Bio-molecule

In all living organisms, enzymes are required for the synthesis of proteins and polynucleotides such as DNA and RNA, which are the components of genes. But since enzymes themselves are proteins, the logical question that must be answered is, Where did the first enzyme come from?

The Statistical Problem

In his book, *Genesis and the Big Bang*, Dr. Gerald L. Schroeder provides a most compelling argument against the random origin of life:

In 1968, Professor Harold Morowitz, a physicist at Yale University, published the book, *Energy Flow in Biology*. Along with other physicists and mathematicians, he had become concerned about the casualness with which some scientists studying the origin of life were assuming that unlikely events must have occurred. These scientists were making assumptions without any attempt to rigorously investigate the probability of such events. Morowitz presented computations of the time required for random chemical reactions to form a bacterium—not an organism as complex as a human, not even a flower, just a simple, single-celled bacterium. Basing his calculations on optimistically rapid rates of reactions, the calculated time for the bacterium to form exceeds not only the 4.5-billion-year age of the Earth, but also the entire 15-billion-year age of the universe.[3]

In his book, *Tornado in a Junkyard*, James Perloff provides us with additional impressive statistical facts against the random formation of biomolecules: "The chances for producing the necessary molecules, amino acids, proteins, et cetera, for a cell one tenth the size of the smallest known to man *(Mycoplasm hominis H. 39)* is less than one in $10^{340,000,000}$ or 10 with 340 million zeros after it."[4]

In his book, *It Couldn't Just Happen*, Lawrence O. Richards states the following:

Since life could not have begun by chance, it must have been purposely created by God. There is no other choice. If one of only two possible choices could not have happened, the other one did!

So never let anyone convince you that it is foolish or "unscientific" to believe in God. The fact is, scientific evidence shows that it is foolish not to believe in God! The evidence truly is on our side!"[5]

The Stereo-specific Problem

Amino acids are the building blocks of proteins. Almost all amino acids can exist in two different stereo-specific forms known as the D and L forms. The D-amino acids are mirror images of the L-amino acids, which means that the D and L have the same spatial relationship to each other as the right hand has to the left hand. Now nineteen of the twenty amino acids found in proteins have the L configuration. All attempts to synthesize amino acids in *vitro* result in the synthesis of a mixture (a racemic modification) of the D and the L forms in equal amounts unless a stereo-specific reaction is employed. However, the use of a stereo-specific reaction would eliminate the condition of randomness. Thus we see that the L-amino acids needed for the synthesis of proteins cannot arise from a random process. From this it should be evident to all that life could *not* have arisen spontaneously from matter, time and chance.

1   Harold G. Coffin, *Creation—Accident or Design?*, Washington D.C.: Review and Herald Publishing Association, 1969, p. 462.
2   Reu E. Hoen, *The Creator and His Workshop*, Mountain View, CA: Pacific Press Publishing Association, 1951, pp. 57–58.
3   Gerald L. Schroeder, Ph.D., *Genesis and the Big Bang*, New York, New York: Bantam Doubleday Dell Publishing Group, Inc., 1990, p.110, 111.
4   James Perloff, *Tornado in a Junkyard*, Arlington, Massachusetts: Refuge Books, 1999, p. 69.
5   Lawrence O. Richards, *It Couldn't Just Happen*, Nashville, TN: Thomas Nelson Inc., 1987, p. 72.

CHAPTER NINE

Some Theories and Philosophies of Origins

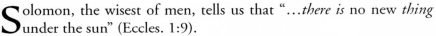

Solomon, the wisest of men, tells us that *"...there is* no new *thing* under the sun"* (Eccles. 1:9).

When we consider several of today's theories of origins, we find that many of them are merely echoes of ancient ideas and philosophies. In this chapter we will briefly review some of these ideas and philosophies, which have come down to us through the ages.

The Philosophy of Greece

Practically all of the philosophical schools of the early Greeks, such as those of Thales of Miletus and Pythagoras of Italy, merged into that of Socrates and then diverged into the school of Plato and Aristotle. Socrates, the greatest of the Greek philosophers, has been called the founder of theistic philosophy.

The School of the Stoics

The School of the Stoics was only one of the many schools of philosophy in Greece during the time of the apostle Paul. There were other schools, such as that of the Epicureans who believed in a life of contentment; the Neopythagoreans who believed that God is good but matter is evil; and the Neoplatonists who had a philosophy touched with emotion.

As some of the philosophers whom Paul encountered on Mars' Hill were Stoics, let us consider a few of the fundamental teachings of Stoicism. This school of philosophy was founded by Zeno, a native of the Levant. He taught his students in the "Painted Porch" in Athens. Stoicism did not approve of the worship of idols and the use of temples, but it approved of polytheism and pantheism, and it taught a form of the resurrection of the dead.

Soper, in his book, *The Religions of Mankind*, states the following: "But it was in respect of morality that the Stoics had a message which reached many of the finest spirits of the age. Good and evil exist side by side, and it is man's part to choose between them.... Sternly he must suppress his impulses and live untouched by any emotional appeals."[1]

Another fundamental doctrine of Stoicism was that "Matter was inseparable from the Deity. He did not create: He only organized. He merely impressed law and order on the substance, which was, in fact, Himself. The manifestation of the universe was only a period in the development of God."[2] These were some of the basic beliefs of the Stoics who disputed with Paul in the Agora of Athens.

The School of the Epicureans

The apostle Paul also met Epicureans in Athens, so let us briefly consider some of the basic tenets of their philosophy.

Conybeare in his book, *Life and Epistles of the Apostle Paul*, writes: "If Stoicism, in its full development, was utterly opposed to Christianity, the same may be said of the very primary principles of the Epicurean school. If the Stoics were pantheists, the Epicureans were virtually atheists."[3] The Epicureans taught that the universe came into being as a result of an accidental interaction of atoms. They believed that nothing should be alarming or disturbing and that man should seek pleasure as he pleases. It is believed that the apostle Paul was quoting the philosophy of the Epicureans when he wrote: "...let us eat and drink; for to-morrow we die" (1 Cor. 15:32).

Paul's Teachings on Origin

On Paul's second missionary tour, he went to Athens after leaving Timothy and Silas in Berea. When he arrived in the capital of heathenism, he was confronted with an array of statues, altars, and temples erected to multitudes of gods. Jealous for the cause of God, he immediately began to proclaim to the Athenians "Jesus and the resurrection" (Acts 17:18). This attack on heathenism culminated in his memorable address on Mars' Hill.

But it was in the Agora, the marketplace of Athens, that Paul met the Stoics of the School of the Painted Porch and the Epicureans of the School of the Garden. In fact, the School of the Painted Porch was in the Agora proper, and that of the Garden was not far away. Here was the place where Demosthenes rebuked the Athenians for their idleness and their obsession for hearing and discussing every new philosophy. In the Agora, Paul reasoned daily with the Athenians who were more than anxious to exercise their dialectics on any subject, especially religion. Born in Tarsus, a city noted for its philosophers, many of whom were Stoics, Paul was prepared for this encounter. In addition, his training at the feet of Gamaliel included many of the works of the Greeks. Gamaliel was one of the most revered of Hebrew teachers. He was known as "the beauty of the law." It is believed that the Epicureans, who were atheists, were the ones who tried to ridicule Paul with the statement, "What will this babbler say?" But the Stoics, who were pantheists, were more tolerant of the apostle Paul and invited him to the Areopagus where he could present his philosophy to the elite of Athens.

According to Greek mythology, the Areopagus was the Hill of Mars (Ares) and it received its name because it was there that Mars (Ares) after he had killed Halirrhothius, Neptune's son, for carrying away his daughter Alcippe, was summoned by Neptune to appear before a tribunal of the judges at night. Mars (Ares) appeared, presented his defense, and was acquitted. Also from this episode, the judges of this highest court in Athens received the name, Areopagite.

The discourse. "Then Paul stood in the midst of Mars' hill, and said, Ye men of Athens, I perceive that in all things ye are too superstitious. For as I passed by, and beheld your devotions, I found an altar with this inscription, TO THE UNKNOWN GOD. Whom therefore ye ignorantly worship, him declare I unto you" (Acts 17: 22–23).

It is believed that the apostle Paul, standing on the top of the Areopagus, was able to see the massive and impressive temples of the

143

Acropolis. Paul pointed his listeners to the temples of the Acropolis crowded with idols and presented to them his philosophy of origin: "God that made the world and all things therein, seeing that he is Lord of heaven and earth, dwelleth not in temples made with hands; Neither is worshipped with men's hands, as though he needed anything, seeing he giveth to all life, and breath, and all things" (Acts 17: 24–25).

And condemning that "age of caste," he reminds his listeners of the Fatherhood of God, and the brotherhood of man, saying: "And hath made of one blood all nations of men for to dwell on all the face of the earth, and hath determined the times before appointed, and the bounds of their habitation; That they should seek the Lord, if haply they might feel after him, and find him, though he be not far from every one of us" (Acts 17: 26–27).

He then reminds them of a statement of one of their own poets:

For in him we live, and move, and have our being; as certain also of your own poets have said, For we are also his offspring. Forasmuch then as we are the offspring of God, we ought not to think that the Godhead is like unto gold, or silver, or stone, graven by art and man's device.

—Acts 17: 28–29

And the times of this ignorance God winked at; but now commandeth all men everywhere to repent: Because he hath appointed a day, in the which he will judge the world in righteousness by *that* man whom he hath ordained; *whereof* he hath given assurance unto all *men*, in that he hath raised him from the dead.

—Acts 17:30–31

At this point in his speech, Paul was interrupted. Some of his listeners broke into laughter, but others courteously told him that they would hear him again about the matter as he spoke about the "resurrection."

In his speech on Mars' Hill, the apostle Paul eloquently met "...science with science, logic with logic, and philosophy with philosophy"[4] as he presented his teachings on origins.

Reconciliation Theories

Over the centuries, a number of attempts have been made to reconcile the Genesis account of creation with the irrefutable evidences from the hard sciences. Let us now consider and evaluate some of the major attempts at reconciliation.

In order to reconcile the Genesis account of creation with the ancient earth theory, the following theories have been proposed:

1. **The Day-Age Theory.** This theory suggests that the days mentioned in Genesis 1 represent long geological periods of time.

Commentary: In chapter four of this book (*Understanding the First Chapter of Genesis*), powerful, linguistic, and scientific arguments were presented supporting the view that the six days of creation week were literal, twenty-four-hour days.

2. **The Multiple-Gap Theory.** In this theory, the days of creation are considered to be twenty-four-hour days which were separated by long geological periods of time.

Commentary: The institution of the Sabbath by the Creator on the seventh day of creation week as stated in Genesis 2:2–3 contradicts this theory: "And on the seventh day God ended his work which he had made; and he rested on the seventh day from all his work which he had made. And God blessed the seventh day, and sanctified it: because that in it he had rested from all his work which God created and made." Also, the specific wording of the fourth commandment of the Decalogue, which is the very foundation of weekly Sabbath observance, negates, contradicts, and refutes this theory: "For in six days the Lord made heaven and earth, the sea, and all that in them is, and rested the seventh day: wherefore the LORD blessed the Sabbath day and hallowed it" (Exod. 20:11).

In the Bible, Sabbath observance can be traced from the seventh day of creation week through the periods of the patriarchs, the judges, and the prophets to the time of Jesus Christ and the apostles. Historically, Sabbath observance can be traced from the time of the apostles to the present time.

3. **The Gap Theory.** According to this theory, it is believed by many scholars that Genesis 1:1–2 describe events that pre-dated the first day of earth's creation week. Others postulate that the earth was initially created in the state ("without form and void") ages before creation week. The best interpretation of Scripture and the irrefutable evidences of science support this theory. (Once more the reader is referred to Chapters 4 and 5 of this book.)

4. **The "Stretching Time" Theory.** Those who support this theory believe that there can be an equivalence between the 15 billion-year age of the universe and the six days of creation week based on Einstein's general theory of relativity and time dilation (the slowing down of clocks at high velocities).

Commentary: This is pure speculation. There is no evidence to support such an absurd idea.

1   E. D. Soper, *The Religions of Mankind,* New York: Abingdon-Cokesbury Press, 1938,
    p. 130.
2   W. J. Conybeare and J. S. Howson, *Life and Epistles of the Apostle Paul,* Grand Rapids: Wm. B. Eerdman's Publishing Company, 1953,
    p. 284.
3   Conybeare and Howson, p. 285.
4   Ellen G. White, *Education,* Mountain View: Pacific Press Publishing Association, 1903, p. 67.

CHAPTER TEN

Macroevolution: Is it Scientifically Valid?

Definitions of Microevolution and Macroevolution

The philosopher Socrates tells us that the definition of terms is the beginning of wisdom. Evolution is one of those terms that must be clearly defined before it can be intelligently discussed. This is so because ninety-nine percent of the time when evolution is being discussed, it is macroevolution rather than microevolution that is the topic of discussion.

Since this is the case, let us clearly define these two terms. *Microevolution* refers to the limited variations or adaptations that can occur within a particular species. An excellent example of this is the development of penicillin-resistant bacteria. Thus, microevolution is a demonstrable, scientific phenomenon. In contrast to microevolution, *macroevolution* is the theory that assumes the random initiation of life forms and the gradual, progressive evolution of complex life forms from simpler life forms. For example, macroevolution teaches the following sequence of development from a primordial soup (rocks and sea water) to simple cells to invertebrates to vertebrates to amphibians to reptiles to birds and mammals to primates and to man. However, it should be noted that not a single transitional form (missing link), living or dead, among these species exists or is known. In his book, *Darwin On Trial*, Phillip

147

Johnson states the following: "'Evolution' can mean anything from the uncontroversial statement that bacteria 'evolve' resistance to antibiotics to the grand metaphysical claim that the universe and mankind 'evolved' entirely by purposeless, mechanical forces."[1]

Evolution—Fact or Theory

Sometime ago during a discussion on the ABC television program *This Week with David Brinkley*, a well-known commentator remarked: "Evolution is a fact." This statement is indicative of how much evolution is misunderstood, even by well-educated people. Even science professors and some of the most ardent proponents of evolutionary philosophy sometimes forget that evolution is a theory and not a fact. Evolution is not a fact. It is a scientific theory.

It should be noted that the first step in the scientific method is the collection of experimental data or facts. In the second step, generalizations or laws are formulated to describe certain relationships based on these facts. The construction of a theory or a theoretical model constitutes the third step. In this context, evolution is merely a theory which should be based on certain laws which should be based on certain facts or observations. Stephen Hawking, the British mathematical physicist considered by some to be the successor to Albert Einstein, provides us with a lucid explanation of the meaning of a scientific theory. In his book, *A Brief History of Time: From the Big Bang to Black Holes*, he writes:

Any physical theory is always provisional, in the sense that it is only a hypothesis: you can never prove it. No matter how many times the results of experiments agree with some theory, you can never be sure that the next time the result will not contradict the theory. On the other hand, you can disprove a theory by finding even a single observation that disagrees with the predictions of the theory.[2]

Genetics and Evolution

Some people believe that genetics provides irrefutable evidence in support of evolution. However, the facts do not support this idea. In commenting on this point, Dr. Harold G. Coffin, author of the book *Creation—Accident or Design?* writes

> It has been said that the science of genetics proves evolution. But the word *evolution* must be defined. If *evolution* merely means change, genetics definitely does support evolution. But if evolution means major change from one basic kind of organism to another basic kind, or progressive change toward ever-increasing complexity, evolution certainly has not been proved by the study of inherited characteristics. This important distinction is usually overlooked completely, and is not mentioned in connection with assertions regarding the evolutionary theory. ...Thus believers in mechanistic evolution disregard accepted scientific principles, and are actually unscientific.[3]

Ten Powerful Scientific Arguments Against Evolution

I. The origin of the universe refutes evolution.

The two most profound questions that the human mind can contemplate are: "Does God exist?" and "What is the origin of the universe?" It is interesting to note that the Book of Genesis begins with the answers to these two questions: In the beginning, God created the heaven and the earth. Genesis 1:1 affirms the existence of a transcendent God who created the universe. When Bertrand Russell, the agnostic English philosopher and mathematician, was asked the question: "Where did the universe come from?" the only response that he could give was, "The universe is just there." To acknowledge that the universe had a beginning is to acknowledge that there was a creation, which was brought about by a creator.

According to big bang cosmology, our universe emerged from an infinitesimally small, infinitely dense, primordial atom. However, evolution cannot explain the origin of this primordial atom. Some creationists believe that at the moment of the big bang (about 15 billion years ago) a transcendent God created energy, matter, space, and time and the fundamental forces of physics, which are gravity, electromagnetism, and the color force (the nuclear strong force and the nuclear weak force).

The Bible also speaks of two kinds of creation: fiat creation and creation ex nihilo.

Fiat creation literally means "creation by command."

The Psalmist David speaks eloquently of the creation of the universe by means of fiat creation: "By the word of the Lord were the heavens made; and all the host of them by the breath of his mouth. For he spake, and it was done; he commanded, and it stood fast" (Ps. 33: 6, 9). "Let them praise the name of the LORD: for he commanded, and they were created" (Ps. 148:5).

The Latin expression, *ex nihilo,* literally means out of nothing. Therefore creation ex nihilo means "creation out of nothing." And we are indebted to the apostle Paul for the concept of creation ex nihilo: "Through faith we understand that the worlds were framed by the word of God, so that things which are seen were not made of things which do appear" (Heb. 11:3).

II. The origin of life refutes evolution.

Evolutionists believe that life is the product of matter, time and chance. However, during the nineteenth century, the great French chemist, Louis Pasteur, demonstrated convincingly and unequivocally that the spontaneous generation of life is impossible.

In his book, *Creation—Accident or Design?*, Dr. Harold Coffin states the following: "Mechanistic evolution requires exceptions to two fundamental laws of biology—that living things develop only from living things, and that they produce offspring basically similar to themselves."[3]

It should be noted that no one has ever observed the process from inanimate to animate (from death to life) except observers of miraculous resurrections. But the opposite process from animate to inanimate (from life to death) is ubiquitously pervasive. The statement that life can only come from a living source or that life can come only from pre-existing life is as much a law as is Newton's law of universal gravitation.

The following is a list of some insurmountable barriers to the spontaneous generation of life:

A. The problem of an initial pre-curser bio-molecule. In all living organisms, enzymes are required for the synthesis of proteins and polynucleotides such as DNA and RNA, which are the components of genes. But since enzymes themselves are proteins, the logical question that must be answered is, Where did the first enzyme come from?

B. The statistical problem. In his book, *Genesis and the Big Bang*, Dr. Gerald L. Schroeder provides a most compelling argument against the random origin of life:

> In 1968, Professor Harold Morowitz, a physicist at Yale University, published the book *Energy Flow in Biology*. Along with other physicists and mathematicians, he had become concerned about the casualness with which some scientists studying the origin of life were assuming that unlikely events must have occurred. These scientists were making assumptions without any attempt to rigorously investigate the probability of such events. Morowitz presented computations of the time required for random chemical reactions to form a bacterium—not an organism as complex as a human, not even a flower, just a simple, single-celled bacterium. Basing his calculations on optimistically rapid rates of reactions, the calculated time for the bacterium to form exceeds not only the 4.5-billion-year age of the Earth, but also the entire 15-billion-year age of the universe.[4]

Statisticians have calculated that the probability of an enzyme coming into existence as a result of randomness is less than 1 in 10^{280}. Remember that the probability of one chance in a trillion, when expressed in scientific notation, would be 1 in 10^{12}.

C. The Stereo-specific problem. Amino acids are the building blocks of proteins. Almost all amino acids can exist in two different stereo-specific forms known as the D and L forms. The D-amino acids are mirror images of the L-amino acids, which means that the D and L have the same spatial relationship to each other as the right hand has to the left hand. Now 19 of the 20 amino acids found in proteins have the L configuration. All attempts to synthesize amino acids in *vitro* result in the synthesis of a mixture (a racemic modification) of the D and the L forms in equal amounts unless a stereo-specific reaction is employed. However, the use of a stereo-specific reaction would eliminate the condition of randomness. Thus we see that the L-amino acids needed for the synthesis of proteins cannot arise from a random process.

From this it should be evident to all that life could not have arisen spontaneously from matter, time and chance.

III. The Anthropic Principle Refutes Evolution.

In the fall of 1973, at an international scientific meeting celebrating the five hundredth anniversary of the birth of Nicolaus Copernicus, Brandon Carter, a cosmologist from Cambridge University and a colleague of Stephen Hawking, presented a paper that would forever demolish the concept of a random universe which came into existence without the intervention of a Creator-God. The title of his paper was "Large Number Coincidences and the Anthropic Principle in Cosmology." According to the anthropic (*anthropos*, Greek "man") principle, all of the physical constants and other parameters of the universe appear to have been carefully, accurately, and precisely chosen or designed to make possible the existence of human life on Planet Earth. Indeed, the universe seems to have been made for man and not man for the universe.

In his excellent book, *God The Evidence*, Patrick Glynn presents the following litany of some of the coincidences presented by Brandon Carter:

Even the most minor tinkering with the value of the fundamental forces of physics—gravity, electromagnetism, the nuclear strong force, or the nuclear weak force would have resulted in an unrecognizable universe: a universe consisting entirely of helium, a universe without protons or atoms, a universe without stars, or a universe that collapsed back in upon itself before the first moments of its existence were up. Changing the precise ratios of the masses of subatomic particles in relation to one another would have similar effects. Even such basics of life as carbon and water depend upon uncanny "fine-tuning" at the subatomic level, strange coincidences in values for which physicists had no other explanation. To take just a few examples:

1. Gravity is roughly 10^{39} times weaker than electromagnetism. If gravity had been 10^{33} times weaker than electromagnetism, "stars would be a billion times less massive and would burn a million times faster."

2. The nuclear weak force is 10^{28} times the strength of gravity. Had the weak force been slightly weaker, all the hydrogen in the universe would have been turned to helium (making water impossible, for example).

3. A stronger nuclear strong force (by as little as 2 percent) would have prevented the formation of protons—yielding a universe without atoms. Decreasing it by 5 percent would have given us a universe without stars.

4. If the difference in mass between a proton and a neutron were not exactly as it is—roughly twice the mass of an electron—then all neutrons would have become protons or vice versa. Say good-bye to chemistry as we know it—and to life.

5. The synthesis of carbon—the vital core of all organic molecules—on a significant scale involves what scientists view as an "astonishing" coincidence in the ratio of the strong force to electromagnetism. This ratio makes it possible for carbon-12 to reach an excited state of exactly 7.65 MeV at the temperature typical of the center of stars, which creates a resonance involving helium-4, beryllium-8, and carbon-12—allowing the necessary binding to take place during a tiny window of opportunity 10^{-17} seconds long.[5]

For a comprehensive listing of these coincidences, the reader is referred to John Leslie's excellent and informative book, *Universes.*

Thus, we see that the anthropic principle, based on the strange coincidences listed above, speaks convincingly and eloquently of a universe created with an incredible degree of order, precision and design in its structure.

Listen to what some famous scientists have said about the big bang and the anthropic principle.

Fred Hoyle: "The big bang theory requires a recent origin of the universe that openly invites the concept of creation."[6] "A common sense interpretation of the facts suggests that a super-intellect has monkeyed with physics, as well as with chemistry and biology, and that there are no blind forces worth speaking about in nature. The numbers one calculates from the facts seem to me so overwhelming as to put this conclusion almost beyond question."[7]

Barry Parker: "If we accept the big bang theory, and most cosmologists now do, then a 'creation' of some sort is forced upon us."[6]

George Smoot: "There is no doubt that a parallel exists between the big bang as an event and the Christian notion of creation from nothing."[6]

Robert Jastrow: "For the scientist who has lived by his faith in the power of reason, the story ends like a bad dream. He has scaled the mountains of ignorance; he is about to conquer the highest peak; as he pulls himself over the final rock, *he is greeted by a band of theologians who have been sitting there for centuries* [emphasis added]."[7]

IV. The fossil record refutes evolution.

The absence of *any* fossils of traditional intermediates between species is the "Achilles heel" of the evolutionary theory. Evolution postulates the continuous progression of life forms from simple cells to invertebrates to vertebrates to amphibians to reptiles to birds and mammals to primates and to man. However, not a single fossil of an intermediate species missing link has ever been found. In his book, *Genesis and the Big Bang*, Dr. Gerald Schroeder states the following:

> The fossil record of the mid-1800s, the time of Darwin's, *On The Origin of Species*, indeed contained organisms ranging from the primitive to the complex. But there was no continuity within this record. With its gaps in fossil evidence, it did *not* demonstrate an evolutionary flow from the primitive to the complex. Darwin realized this and acknowledged the deficiency…. The intense paleontological efforts of the past hundred years have not produced the evidence…. As Dr. Niles Eldredge of the American Museum of Natural History in New York stated so definitively, "The pattern [in the fossil record] that we were told to find for the past one hundred and twenty years does not exist…. The theory of evolution is unsubstantiated by the fossil record."[8]

In a vain attempt to apologize for the absence of fossils of transitional forms, evolutionists like Stephen Jay Gould and Niles Eldredge concocted the concept of punctuated equilibrium. In this theory, they postulated the sudden appearance of new species in the evolutionary record. They did this in the absence of any evidence whatsoever to support their ideas.

Concerning punctuated equilibrium, Dr. Phillip E. Johnson states the following in his book, *Darwin on Trial*:

> The fossil record was revisited in the 1970s in works by Stephen Jay Gould, Niles Eldredge, and Steven Stanley. Gould and Eldredge proposed a new theory they called "punctuated equilibrium" ("punk eek" to the irreverent), to deal with an embarrassing fact: the fossil record today on the whole looks very much as it did in 1859, despite the fact that an enormous amount of fossil hunting has gone on in the intervening years. In the words of Gould: "The history of most fossil species includes two features particularly inconsistent with gradualism: Stasis. Most species exhibit no directional change during their tenure on earth. They appear in the fossil record looking pretty much the same as when they disappear.... Sudden appearance. In any local area, a species does not arise gradually by the steady transformation of its ancestors; it appears all at once and 'fully formed.'
>
> "In short, if evolution means the gradual change of one kind of organism into another kind, the outstanding characteristic of the fossil record is the absence of evidence for evolution."[9]

The questionable ages of fossils refute evolution. Evolutionists make the false assumption that the age of a fossil is the same as that of the rock bearing the fossil. However, there is no scientific basis to support this assumption.

Those evolutionists who believe that life on planet earth can be measured in millions of years base their position on the age of minerals associated with fossils. They make the unsupported assumption that the age of the fossil is the same as the age of the mineral. Dr. Robert H. Brown of the Geoscience Research Institute demolishes this position by pointing out the error that evolutionists make when they assume that the age of the fossil is identical to the age of the mineral associated with it:

> The second area of evidence that should be mentioned here is the radiometric data concerning inorganic minerals associated with fossils. It has been commonly assumed that the radiometric "clocks" in

these minerals were "set zero" when the mineral was brought into association with a fossil. This assumption is overly simplistic. It has not been scrutinized as it should have been, because it provides ages for fossils that appear to give support for the evolutionary viewpoint that became popular decades before radiometric-dating techniques were developed."[10]

Lawrence O. Richards, author of the book, *It Couldn't Just Happen,* states the following:

There are other problems for people who look at the fossil record to find evidence for the theory of evolution. So much of what is found just does not fit. Rock strata often do not fit together as they should. Sometimes "older" rocks are found on "younger" rocks, with no evidence they were jumbled or turned over. In some places rock strata will skip whole geologic eras, with rock supposedly millions of years younger laid directly on rock millions of years older, as though nothing had happened at that place for ages.

Fossils are also found out of order. In some places fossil trees extend through rock strata supposedly laid down millions of years apart."[11]

V. The Principle of Irreducible Complexity Refutes Evolution.

According to Michael Behe, the principle of irreducible complexity states that a biological structure (e.g., eye) or process (e.g., clotting) requires the presence of all components in order to function. Therefore, such structures and processes could not have evolved in incremental stages. For example, the major components of the eye are the sclera, the cornea, the iris, the pupil, the optic nerve, and the Ciliary tissues. And the major components of the clotting process are prothrombin, thrombin, fibrinogen, and a number of required clotting factors.

If Charles Darwin were alive today and had the knowledge of modern science, he would be among the first to repudiate his theory of evolution. Listen to his own words: "If it could be demonstrated that any complex organ existed which could not possibly have been formed by numerous, successive, slight modifications, my theory would absolutely break down."[12]

In his book, *Darwin's Black Box*, Dr. Michael Behe states the following:

Darwin knew that his theory of gradual evolution by natural selection carried a heavy burden…. From Mivart's concern over the incipient stages of new structures to Margulis's dismissal of gradual evolution, critics of Darwin have suspected that his criterion of failure had been met…. Since natural selection can only choose systems that are already working, then if a biological system cannot be produced gradually it would have to arise as an integrated unit, in one fell swoop, for natural selection to have anything to act on.[13]

VI. The Second Law of Thermodynamics Refutes Evolution.

The second law of thermodynamics is one of the most revered laws in all of science. One form of this law states that a spontaneous reaction or process leads to an increase in entropy or disorder. Based on this law, a spontaneous evolutionary process should result in greater entropy or disorder. Therefore the assumption that the spontaneous accidental interaction of atoms (disorder) could lead to the formation of highly structured compounds (order) violates the second law of thermodynamics.

VII. The Existence of Living Fossils Refutes Evolution.

The existence of living fossils, which do not show any evidence of evolution and which should have become extinct ages ago, is an embarrassment to the theory of evolution. Dr. Harold G. Coffin beautifully articulates this problem as follows:

Another interesting category of organism is the so-called "living fossils," plants and animals that were supposed to have been extinct for at least several millions of years, but which have been found to be alive and thriving somewhere in the world. It is difficult for the evolutionary paleontologist to understand how an animal existing since Paleozoic times could have left no trace of itself in the rocks since, for example the Devonian period. He is also bothered by the fact that there may be little evidence of evolutionary change between the Devonian specimens and the recent ones. The creationist is not bothered, because he counts no more than a few thousand years since the organism was incorporated into the fossil record.[14]

VIII. The Origin of Genetic Information Refutes Evolution.

Molecular biology tells us that the genetic information that directs biological processes is encoded in the DNA, which is a subunit of genes.

The first gene, with its DNA component(s) was either created or came into existence as a result of randomness. Today we know that enzymes are required for the synthesis of DNA. It is also a known fact that enzymes are proteins whose syntheses must be directed by specific genes (DNA). The question that evolutionists must answer is this: Which came first—the DNA (which requires enzymes for its synthesis) or the enzyme, which is a protein [which requires genes (DNA) for its synthesis]? If their answer is the DNA, then they must explain how such a highly structured biomolecule with specific encoded information could have arisen as a result of randomness. In other words, they must explain how information could come from non-information or how sense could come from non-sense spontaneously. Someone has said that there are approximately 600,000 pages of information in a single strand of DNA. (See the insurmountable barriers to the spontaneous generation of life found under argument 2 above.)

Dr. Harold Morowitz, a physicist at Yale University and author of the book, *Energy Flow in Biology*, has calculated the amount of time required for the process of randomness to produce a single bacterium. He found that it would require more time than the age of the universe (15 billion years or 10^{18} seconds) for such a process to be completed. This means that more time would be required for randomness to work than the amount of time that ever existed, assuming that time began when the universe was created according to big bang cosmology.

IX. Intelligent Design Refutes Evolution

The answer to the fundamental question of origins comes either from intelligent design or from the creed of the evolutionist—matter, time and chance. No other possibility is known. There is no middle ground.

The advocates of intelligent design, of course believe in the existence of a transcendent, creator-God who brought the universe and man into existence. They believe that underlying all physical phenomena is a transcendent substratum of design.

Supporters of intelligent design take comfort in the fact that intelligent design is ubiquitously pervasive in nature. Even the great British evolutionist, Richard Dawkins, concedes this in his book, *The Blind Watchmaker*. Listen to his own words:

> Biology…is the study of complicated things that give the appearance of having been designed for a purpose…. Natural Selection is the blind watchmaker, blind because it does not see ahead, does not plan consequences, has no purpose in view. Yet the living results of natural selection overwhelmingly impress us with the appearance of design as if by a master watchmaker, impress us with the illusion of design and planning.[15]

Even though Dawkins admits to the pervasive existence of design in nature, he makes the monumental mistake of attributing this design to natural selection. Even the title of his book is an oxymoron because blind watchmakers do not exist (i.e. if a man is blind, he is not a watchmaker; and if he is a watchmaker, he is not blind). Another monumental mistake that Dawkins made is his failure to recognize the limitations of natural selection. In the evolutionary process, natural selection can only change an organism. It cannot create a new organism.

The water molecule—a classical example of intelligent design. The angular shape of the water molecule is responsible for most of its characteristic properties. For example, if the water molecule were linear, water under normal living conditions would be a gas and not a liquid. If water were a gas, there would be no oceans, lakes, rivers or streams. More than 70 percent by weight of the human body is water, and water is a major component of all plants and animals. Therefore, *life as we know it* on planet Earth would be non-existent if the water molecule were linear and not angular. Based on these facts, I would like to state my hydromorphic principle as follows: The form of life on planet Earth is a function of the shape of the water molecule.

In chemistry we learn that the formation of a molecule of water involves the overlapping of two atomic orbitals of the oxygen atom by the atomic orbitals of two hydrogen atoms. The two atomic orbitals of oxygen that are involved in bonding are designed to be are about 109.5 degrees apart. This design feature is primarily responsible for the angular shape of the molecule in which the two hydrogen atoms are 105 degrees apart. When one considers that the number of bonding atomic orbitals that an oxygen atom possesses is a consequence not only of its component subatomic particles (8 protons, 8 neutrons and 8 electrons) but is also a consequence of its electronic configuration and the application and restriction of such rules as Pauli's exclusion principle and Hund's rule of maximum multiplicity, it is evident that this structure is the result of design and not of randomness. If, after considering this classical example of intelligent design, someone still wants to believe that our being and our existence are the result of randomness, then I have a bridge in Brooklyn that I would like to sell to him.

Note: The most elementary form of Pauli's exclusion principle states that no two electrons in an atom can have the same energy. The application of this principle determines the electron configuration of atoms. Likewise, Hund's rule of maximum multiplicity dictates the orbital diagram, or the order in which electrons can enter atomic orbitals in a particular sub-shell of an atom.

The following are some of the important chemical and physical properties of water which are largely due to its angular shape:

Its dipole moment
Its hydrogen bonding ability
Its higher than expected boiling point
Its high heat of fusion
Its high heat of vaporization, and
Its unusual density changes.

The importance of the unique density changes in water can be appreciated when one considers that if water did not become lighter on freezing, lakes would freeze from the bottom up (instead of from the surface), and thus freeze completely and eliminate aquatic life.

X. The Scientific Method Refutes Evolution.

Science is usually pursued by means of the scientific method. This method can be summarized in the following three steps:

The collection of experimental data. This is done by observation or experimentation.

The formation of a law. From the data collected, certain regularities or relationships may become apparent that can be codified into a law. A law in science is merely a "coherent, economy-of-thought" description of the way things behave.

The construction of a model. In this final step, a hypothesis or a scientific guess is constructed by entertaining certain assumptions or postulates that are consistent with the data, with the law, and with each other. If this hypothesis can be used to predict other relationships that can be experimentally verified, and if it is consistent with subsequently discovered facts, it may, in due time, be promoted to the status of a *theory* or *model*. It should be clearly understood that a theory can never be proved. Experimental results that confirm predictions based on the theory merely validate the theory but do not prove the theory. Experimental results that do not harmonize with the theory usually result in some modification of the theory. A theory is not a scientific fact. It is simply a useful device for explaining natural phenomena.

When Charles Darwin formulated his theory of the origin of species in the mid-nineteenth century he made the monumental mistake of extending his observations of microevolution (variations within species) to the yet unproven, nonexistent phenomenon of macroevolution (the transformation of one species into another). In searching for evidence for macroevolution, Darwin studied the fossil record, but there was no evidence to support his ideas of macroevolution in the fossil record. In the absence of evidence to support his hypothesis he then assumed that the fossil record was incomplete because of the absence of fossils of transitional forms (missing links). In order to save his theory, he entertained the notion that the fossil record was incomplete, and that further explorations and discoveries of fossils would provide the evidence that was lacking. However, after 150 years of searching the fossil record, there is still no evidence to support macroevolution. As a result of this failure, committed evolutionists like Stephen Jay Gould, Niles Eldridge, and Steven Stanley had to invent the concept of punctuated equilibrium in a vain attempt to explain the absence of transitional forms in the fossil record. Thus, we see that macroevolution fails the first step in the scientific method, which is observations that can lead to laws and then to a valid scientific theory.

Testimonies of Scientists

In his most interesting book, *Tornado in a Junkyard*, the author James Perloff provides us with the following views of some reputable scientists concerning the failures of the theory of evolution:

Kenneth Hsu wrote in the *Journal of Sedimentary Petrology* (1896): "We have all heard of *The Origin of the Species*, although few of us have had time to read it; I did not secure a copy until two years ago. A casual perusal of the classic made me understand the rage of Paul Feyerabend.... I agree with him that Darwinism contains 'wicked lies'; it is not a 'natural law' formulated on the basis of factual evidence, but a dogma, reflecting social philosophy of the last century."

Swedish biologist Søren Løvtrup said in 1987: "I believe that one day the Darwinian myth will be ranked the greatest deceit in the history of science."

Over the years, other scientists have renounced evolution—or were never fooled to begin with. Sir John William Dawson, who pioneered Canadian geology and served as president of both McGill University and the British Association for the Advancement of Science, said: "This evolutionist doctrine is itself one of the strangest phenomena of humanity...a system destitute of any shadow of proof, and supported merely by vague analogies and figures of speech.... Now no one pretends that they rest on facts actually observed, for no one has ever observed the production of even one species.... Let the reader take up either of Darwin's great books, or Spencer's 'Biology,' and merely ask himself as he reads each paragraph, 'What is assumed here and what is proved?' and he will find the whole fabric melt away like a vision.... We thus see that evolution as an hypothesis has no basis in experience or in scientific fact, and that its imagined series of transmutations has breaks which cannot be filled."

Paul Lemoine, who was president of the Geological Society of France and director of the Natural History Museum in Paris, abandoned evolution. As chief editor of the *Encyclopedie Française*, 1937 edition, he wrote in that work: "The theory of evolution is impossible. At base, in spite of appearances, no one any longer believes in it.... Evolution is a kind of dogma which the priests no longer believe, but which they maintain for their people."

Dr. T.N. Tahmisian of the U.S. Atomic Energy Commission said in 1959: "Scientists who go about teaching that evolution is a fact of life are great con-men, and the story they are telling may be the greatest hoax ever. In explaining evolution, we do not have one iota of fact."

Zoologist Albert Fleischmann of the University of Erlangen declared: "The Darwinian theory of descent has not a single fact to confirm it in the realm of nature. It is not the result of scientific research, but purely the product of imagination." He explained: "The theory suffers from grave defects, which are becoming more and more apparent as time advances. It can no longer square with practical scientific knowledge, nor does it suffice for our theoretical grasp of the facts. ...No one can demonstrate that the limits of a species have ever been passed. These are the Rubicons which evolutionists cannot cross.... Darwin ransacked other spheres of practical research work for ideas. In particular, he borrowed his views on selection from T.R. Malthus' ideas regarding the dangers of overpopulation, to which he added the facts recorded by breeders.... But his whole resulting scheme remains, to this day, foreign to scientifically established zoology, since actual changes of species by such means are still unknown." (p. 118)

Louis Bounoure, former director of the Strasbourg Zoological Museum and later director of research at the French National Center of Scientific Research, stated in 1984: "Evolutionism is a fairy tale for grown-ups. This theory has helped nothing in the progress of science. It is useless."

Dr. Wolfgang Smith, who taught at MIT and UCLA, and has written on a wide spectrum of scientific topics, said in 1988: "And the salient fact is this: *if by evolution we mean macroevolution (as we henceforth shall), then it can be said with the utmost rigor that the doctrine is totally bereft of scientific sanction.* Now, to be sure, given the multitude of extravagant claims about evolution promulgated by evolutionists with an air of scientific infallibility, this may indeed sound strange. And yet the fact remains that there exists to this day not a shred of *bona fide* scientific evidence in support of the thesis that macroevolutionary transformations have ever occurred."

One of the most startling quotations comes from Colin Patterson, senior paleontologist at the British Museum of Natural History....

Here are Patterson's remarks:

"One of the reasons I started taking this antievolutionary view, or let's call it a non-evolutionary view, was last year I had a sudden realization for over twenty years I had thought I was working on evolution in some way. One morning I woke up and something had happened in the night, and it struck me that I had been working on this stuff for twenty years and there was not one thing I knew about it. That's quite a shock that one can be misled for so long. Either there was something wrong with me or there was something wrong with evolutionary theory. Naturally, I knew there was nothing wrong with me, so for the last few years I've tried putting a simple question to various people and groups of people.

"Question is: Can you tell me anything you know about evolution, any one thing that is true? I tried that question on the geology staff at the Field Museum of Natural History and the only answer I got was silence. I tried it on the members of the Evolutionary Morphology seminar in the University of Chicago, a very prestigious body of evolutionists, and all I got there was silence for a long time and eventually one person said, 'I do know one thing—that it ought not to be taught in high school.'"[16]

For Further Study

The following is a brief list of some of the books by reputable scholars that question the scientific validity of the theory of evolution:

Michael Behe, *Darwin's Black Box.* Dr. Michael Behe is a professor of Biochemistry at Lehigh University.

Neil Broom, *How Blind is the Watchmaker?* Neil Broom is an associate professor in the department of chemical and materials engineering at The University of Auckland in New Zealand.

Michael Denton, *Evolution: A Theory in Crisis.* Michael Denton is a distinguished molecular biologist and physician.

Duane T. Gish, *Evolution: The Fossils Still Say NO!*

Phillip E. Johnson, *Darwin On Trial.*

Phillip E. Johnson, *Defeating Darwinism by Opening Minds.*

Phillip E. Johnson, *Reason in the Balance.* Attorney Phillip Johnson is a member of the Law School Faculty at the University of California—Berkeley.

Martin Lubenow, *Bones of Contention.*

James Perloff, *Tornado in a Junkyard.* James Perloff is a freelance writer and a former contributing editor to *The New American.*

1   Phillip E. Johnson, *Darwin On Trial,* Illinois: InterVarsity Press, 1993, p. 9.

2   Stephen Hawking, *A Brief History of Time: From the Big Bang to Black Holes,* New York: Bantam, 1990, p. 10.

3   Harold G. Coffin, *Creation—Accident or Design?,* Washington, D.C.: Review and Herald Publishing Association, 1969, pp. 458–459.

4   Gerald L. Schroeder, Ph.D., *Genesis and the Big Bang,* New York, New York: Bantam Doubleday Dell Publishing Group, Inc., 1990, pp.110, 111.

5   Patrick Glynn, *GOD The Evidence,* Rocklin, CA: Prima Publishing, 1997, pp.28–30.

6   Erwin W. Lutzer, *Seven Reasons Why You Can Trust The Bible,* Chicago: Moody Press, 1998, p. 139.

7   Ibid., p.151.

8   Gerald L. Schroeder, Ph.D., *Genesis and the Big Bang,* New York, New York: Bantam Doubleday Dell Publishing Group, Inc., 1990, p. 134.

9   Phillip E. Johnson, *Darwin On Trial*, Illinois: InterVarsity Press, 1993, p. 50.

10 Robert H. Brown, *How Old is the World*, Review and Herald, Washington D. C.: Review and Herald Publishing Association, 1975, p. 8.

11 Lawrence O. Richards, *It Couldn't Just Happen*, Nashville, TN: Thomas Nelson, Inc., 1987, p. 89.

12 Charles Darwin (1872) *Origin of Species*, 6th ed. (1988), New York University Press, p. 154.

13 Michael Behe, *Darwin's Black Box*, New York, New York: Simon &Schuster, Inc., 1996, p. 39.

14 Harold G. Coffin, *Creation—Accident or Design?*, Washington, D.C.: Review and Herald Publishing Association, 1969, pp. 458–459.

15 Phillip E. Johnson, *Darwin On Trial*, Illinois: InterVarsity Press, 1993, p. 168.

16 James Perloff, *Tornado in a Junkyard*, Arlington, MA: Refuge Books, 1999, pp. 117–119.

Epilogue

Introduction

"O ut of zeal and love for the elucidation of the truth the following theses will be debated" (Preamble to Luther's 95 Theses).

In the spirit that motivated Martin Luther to nail his 95 Theses to the church doors at Wittenberg, this epilogue is written.

Since the views expressed by the author in this book are diametrically opposed to those of the young earth creationists as well as to those of the theistic evolutionists (progressive creationists) and the non-theistic evolutionists, the author wishes to briefly and clearly summarize *his views* on the creation of the universe, its chronology, the origin of life, and the theory of macroevolution.

Creation of the Universe

(See Chapter 4 for supporting statements.)

The first two verses of Genesis 1 describe the creation of the universe including terrestrial matter.

There was an obvious gap between the events described in verses one and two and the beginning of creation week as described in verse three.

It should be noted that the six days of creation week are all punctuated with the expression, "Let there be...." This marks off creation week from the period of time (pre-day one) that preceded it.

The six days mentioned in the fourth commandment of the Decalogue refer to the creative events of creation week. "For in six days the LORD made heaven and earth, the sea, and all that in them is, and rested the seventh day: wherefore the Lord blessed the Sabbath day, and hallowed it" (Exod. 20:11).

The "heaven" in this commandment refers to the atmospheric heavens created on the second day of creation week; "the earth" and "the seas" refer to the dry land and the seas created on the third day of creation week, and "all that in them is" refers to the vegetation created on the third day of creation week and the fishes, etc., created on the fifth day of creation week. Thus we see that the fourth commandment speaks specifically about the creative events that took place on the second, the third, and the fifth days of creation week. Therefore, "the six days" of the fourth commandment apply to the six days of creation week rather than to the time period for the creation of the universe.

A Chronology of the Creation of the Universe
(See Chapter 5 for supporting statement.)
1. Creation of the universe. At the moment of creation, "in the beginning," an eternal, transcendent, omnipotent, omniscient Creator-God created energy, matter, the dimensions of space and time, and the fundamental forces of physics, which are gravity, electromagnetism, and the color force (the nuclear strong force and the nuclear weak force) when He created the universe.
2. Formation of galaxies, stars, and planets. In the course of time the Creator formed the cosmic matter that was created "in the beginning" into galaxies, stars, planets and habitable worlds.
3. Creation of the angels and other heavenly beings. Long before the creation of planet earth and man, angels and other heavenly beings were created.

4. The fall of Lucifer. Sometime before the creation of planet Earth and man, Lucifer was cast out of heaven.

5. Postponement of the creation of planet Earth and man. Some Bible commentators believe that the creation of man on planet earth had to be postponed until Lucifer's rebellion had "ripened into open revolt."

6. Condition of planet Earth before creation week. Genesis 1:2 describes the condition of the earth prior to the first day of creation week.

7. Creation week for planet Earth. During this week terrestrial matter (without form and void) was organized into a habitable world.

Expansion of the Universe and Big Bang Cosmology
(See Chapter 6 for supporting statements.)

Since the question, What is the origin of the universe? lies at the interface of both science and religion, the author believes that we can get closer to the truth if we combine the unequivocal testimony of the Bible with the irrefutable facts of the hard sciences. In this book the author has endeavored to accomplish this without compromising the testimony of the Bible or the evidences of science.

The following are a few examples of the irrefutable facts of science that support the concept of an expanding universe, a concept that is an important part of big bang cosmology:

1. Newton's Law of Universal Gravitation requires the existence of an expanding or a contracting universe.

2. Einstein's general theory of relativity is consistent with an expanding universe. Alexander Friedman, a Russian scientist, and Georges Lemaitre, Belgian astrophysicist and a member of the faculty of the pontifical academy of the Vatican have confirmed this relationship.

3. "The red shift" of receding galaxies (the Doppler principle) is evidence of an expanding universe.

4. Hubble's Law confirms the existence of an expanding universe.

[In evaluating Einstein's general theory of relativity, it should be noted that all of the predictions made by his theory have been confirmed to date by calculation, observation, and experimentation.]

The unequivocal testimony of the Bible, as stated in the following texts, also supports the idea of an expanding universe:

He hath made the earth by his power, he hath established the world by his wisdom, and hath stretched out the heavens by his discretion.

—Jer 10:12

He hath made the earth by his power, he hath established the world by his wisdom, and hath stretched out the heaven by his understanding.

—Jer. 51:15

Thus saith God the LORD, he that created the heavens and stretched them out....

—Isa. 42:5

I have made the earth, and created man upon it: I, *even* my hands, have stretched out the heavens, and all their hosts have I commanded.

—Isa. 45:12

Mine hand also hath laid the foundation of the earth, and my right hand hath spanned the heavens: when I call unto them they stand up together.

—Isa. 48:13

It is He that sitteth on the circle of the earth...that stretcheth out the heavens as a curtain, and spreadeth them out as a tent to dwell in.

—Isa. 40:22

Who coverest thyself with light as with a garment: who stretchest out the heavens like a curtain.

—Ps.104:2

Which alone spreadeth out the heavens....

—Job 9:8

The Origin of Life on Planet Earth

(See Chapter 8 for supporting statements.)

The apostle Paul, in his famous speech on Mars' hill refers to God as the source of all life. (See Acts 17:24–25.)

The great French Chemist, Louis Pasteur demonstrated unequivocally that the spontaneous generation of life does not occur.

The statement that life can come only from a life source or that life can come only from pre-existing life is as much a law as is Newton's law of universal gravitation. In science a law is considered to be an "economy-of-thought" description of the way nature behaves. Thus, Newton's law of universal gravitation is a description of the way nature behaves. For thousands of years before Newton codified or articulated his law of universal gravitation, the consequences of Newton's law of universal gravitation were observed. It was noted without exception, that all bodies heavier than air and lacking a propulsion system of their own would fall to the earth. Likewise, for thousands of years up until the present time, it has been observed in nature, without exception, that life comes only from a source of life (life source). This statement is as valid a law as is Newton's law of universal gravitation. No one has ever observed the process from inanimate to animate (from death to life), except observers of miraculous resurrections or restorations of life. But the opposite process from animate to inanimate (from life to death) is ubiquitously pervasive.

Dr. Harold Morowitz, a physicist at Yale University and author of the book, *Energy Flow in Biology*, has calculated the amount of time required for the process of randomness to produce a single bacterium. He found that it would require more time than the age of the universe (15 billion years or 10^{18} seconds) for such a process to be completed. This means that more time would be required for randomness to work than the amount of time that ever existed, assuming that time began when the universe was created according to big bang cosmology.

In his book, *It Couldn't Just Happen*, Lawrence O. Richards states the following:

> Since life could not have begun by chance, it must have been purposely created by God. There is no other choice. If one of only two possible choices could not have happened, the other one did!

So never let anyone convince you that it is foolish or "unscientific" to believe in God. The fact is, scientific evidence shows that it is foolish *not* (emphasis supplied) to believe in God! The evidence truly is on our side!"

Macroevolution Is Not Scientifically Valid

(See chapter 10 for supporting statements.)

Microevolution refers to the limited variations or adaptations that can occur within a particular species. An excellent example of this is the development of penicillin-resistant bacteria. Thus, microevolution is a demonstrable, scientific phenomenon.

In contrast to microevolution, macroevolution is the theory that assumes the random initiation of life forms and the gradual, progressive evolution of complex life forms from simpler life forms. For example, macroevolution teaches the following sequence of development from a primordial soup (rocks and sea water) to simple cells to invertebrates to vertebrates to amphibians to reptiles to birds and mammals to primates and to man. However, it should be noted that not a single transitional form (missing link), living or dead, among these species exists or is known.

Ten Powerful Scientific Arguments Against Macroevolution

I.	The origin of the universe refutes evolution.
II.	The origin of life refutes evolution.
III.	The anthropic principle refutes evolution.
IV.	The fossil record refutes evolution.
V.	The principle of irreducible complexity refutes evolution.
VI.	The second law of thermodynamics refutes evolution.
VII.	The existence of living fossils refutes evolution.
VIII.	The origin of genetic information refutes evolution
IX.	Intelligent design refutes evolution.
X.	The scientific method refutes evolution.

Testimonies of Reputable Scientists

Kenneth Hsu wrote in the *Journal of Sedimentary Petrology* (1896): "...Darwinism contains 'wicked lies'; it is not a 'natural law' formulated on the basis of factual evidence...."

Swedish biologist Søren Løvtrup said in 1987: "I believe that one day the Darwinian myth will be ranked the greatest deceit in the history of science...."

Sir John William Dawson, who pioneered Canadian geology and served as president of both McGill University and the British Association for the Advancement of Science, said: "This evolutionist doctrine is itself one of the strangest phenomena of humanity...a system destitute of any shadow of proof, and supported merely by vague analogies and figures of speech....Now no one pretends that they rest on facts actually observed, for no one has ever observed the production of even species....Let the reader take up either Darwin's great books, or Spencer's 'Biology,' and merely ask himself as he reads each paragraph, 'What is assumed here and what is proved?' and he will find the whole fabric melt away like a vision.... We thus see that evolution as an hypothesis has no basis in experience or in scientific fact, and that its imagined series of transmutations has breaks which cannot be filled...."

Paul Lemoine was president of the Geological Society of France and director of the Natural History Museum in Paris. As chief editor of the *Encyclopedie Française,* 1937 edition, he wrote in that work: "The theory of evolution is impossible. At base, in spite of appearances, no one any longer believes in it.... Evolution is a kind of dogma which the priests no longer believe, but which they maintain for their people...."

Dr. T.N. Tahmisian of the U.S. Atomic Energy Commission said in 1959: "Scientists who go about teaching that evolution is a fact of life are great con-men, and the story they are telling may be the greatest hoax ever. In explaining evolution, we do not have one iota of fact...."

Zoologist Albert Fleischmann of the University of Erlangen declared: "The Darwinian theory of descent has not a single fact to confirm it in the realm of nature. It is not the result of scientific research, but purely the product of imagination...But his whole resulting scheme remains, to this day, foreign to scientifically established zoology, since actual changes of species by such means are still unknown...."

Louis Bounoure, former director of the Strasbourg Zoological Museum and later director of research at the French National Center of Scientific Research, stated in 1984:

"Evolutionism is a fairy tale for grown-ups. This theory has helped nothing in the progress of science. It is useless...."

Dr. Wolfgang Smith, who taught at MIT and UCLA, and has written on a wide spectrum of scientific topics, said in 1988: "And the salient fact is this: *if by evolution we mean macroevolution (as we henceforth shall), then it can be said with the utmost rigor that the doctrine is totally bereft of scientific sanction.* ...And yet the fact remains that there exists to this day not a shred of *bona fide* scientific evidence in support of the thesis that macroevolutionary transformations have ever occurred...."

Colin Paterson, senior paleontologist at the British Museum of Natural History comments: "Question is: Can you tell me anything you know about evolution, any one thing that is true? I tried that question on the geology staff at the Field Museum of Natural History and the only answer I got was silence. I tried it on the members of the Evolutionary Morphology seminar in the University of Chicago, a very prestigious body of evolutionists, and all I got there was silence for a long time and eventually one person said, 'I do know one thing—that it ought not to be taught in high school....'"

Conclusion

This book began with the two most profound questions that the human mind can contemplate: "Does God exist?" and "What is the origin of the universe?" In the pages of this book I have provided a litany of Biblical and scientific evidences for the creation of the universe by a creator-God. I firmly believe that the very existence of the universe is evidence for the existence of a creator-God. The testimony of science on this point is unequivocal. Listen to the words of Sir Isaac Newton, one of the greatest disciples of science:

> This universe exists, and by that one impossible fact declares itself a miracle; postulates an infinite Power within itself, a whole greater than any part: a unity sustaining all, binding all worlds into one.

This is a mystery, the unquestionable miracle that we know, implying every attribute of God."[1]

This most beautiful system of sun, planets, and comets could only proceed from the counsel and dominion of an intelligent and powerful Being. This Being governs all things, not as the soul of the world, but as Lord over all; and on account of His dominion, He is wont to be called Lord God.[2]

Likewise, the testimony of the Bible on this point is unequivocal and is most eloquently expressed by the apostle Paul in his epistle to the Romans: "For the invisible things of him from the creation of the world are clearly seen, being understood by the things that are made, *even* his eternal power and Godhead; so that they are without excuse" (Rom. 1:20).

Finally, the views expressed in this book are those which are solidly based on the unequivocal testimony of the Bible and the irrefutable evidences of the hard sciences, especially Einstein's general theory of relativity. In evaluating Einstein's general theory of relativity, it should be noted that all of the predictions made by his theory have been confirmed to date by calculation, observation and experimentation.

The author firmly believes that big bang cosmology is probably the best explanation conceived by the scientific mind to explain the genesis of the universe.

However, in spite of the overwhelming irrefutable scientific evidence upon which this cosmology is based, and in spite of the consistent, coherent, and cogent scientific logic which undergirds big bang cosmology, the author believes that the big bang is still merely a *possible mechanism* for explaining the genesis of the universe. Let us remember the observation of the Andrade: "Science has proof but no certainty: religion has certainty but no proof."

The only thing that we can be certain about is the testimony of the Creator himself. Listen to His words in the following texts:

In the beginning, God created the heaven and the earth."

—Gen. 1:1

By the word of the Lord were the heavens made; and all the hosts of them by the breadth of his mouth. For he spake and it was *done*, he commanded, and it stood fast.

—Ps. 33:6, 9

In the beginning was the Word, and the Word was with God, and the Word was God. The same was in the beginning with God. All things were made by him; and without him was not any thing made that was made.

—John 1:1–3

Who is the image of the invisible God, the firstborn of every creature: For by him were all things created, that are in heaven, and that are in earth, visible and invisible, whether *they be* thrones, or dominions, or principalities, or powers: all things were created by him, and for him: And he is before all things, and by him all things consist.

—Col. 1:15–17

Through faith we understand that the worlds were framed by the word of God, so that things which are seen were not made of things which do appear.

—Heb. 11:3

Note: The reader is again referred to the Word of Caution stated in the Preface.

---

1   Phillip L. Knox, *Sky Wonders*, Mountain View: Pacific Press Publishing Association, 1945, p. 17.
2   James Kennedy and Jerry Newcomb, *What if Jesus Had Never Been Born?*, Nashville, TN: Thomas Nelson Inc., 1994, p. 100.

Appendix A

Expanding Sheet Theory of Steihardt and Turok

Steinhardt and Turok[1] speculate that the universe can refill with hot, dense matter and energy. They suggest that the universe exists as two infinitely parallel sheets separated by a microscopic distance defined as the fifth dimension. The dense matter and energy in the sheets expand in all directions, gradually spreading out and dispersing matter and energy. Once the matter and energy dissipate, the sheets stop stretching and move toward each other as the fifth dimension collapses. At this point the sheets bounce off each other causing them to be charged with hot and dense matter and a process analogous to the big bang occurs.

Around the mid twentieth century, the big bang theory was proposed to explain the origin of the universe. Later, the theory of inflation was added to the big bang theory in order to explain the "smoothness and homogeneity" of the universe and the tiny ripples in space that led to the formation of galaxies. Steinhardt and Turok's new model replaces inflation and dark energy with an energy field that also explains the smoothness, homogeneity and ripples in the universe. This model includes a prediction of the future course of the universe. Whereas, the big bang theory is not able to do this.

It seems appropriate to suggest that some kind of relation exists between the energy field that pervades the universe and the power of

God. God is the unifying entity who controls all processes related to creation. The *expanding sheet theory* (an alternative to the big bang theory) is a reasonable model for understanding the creation of the universe for within this theory is the embodiment of the ever-pervading power of God in the form of matter and energy.

---

1   http://www.sciencedaily.com/releases/2002/04/020429080540.htm

Appendix B

Description of the Flood

In her book, *Patriarchs and Prophets*, the noted Bible commentator E.G. White provides us with a very plausible and picturesque description of the earth before the Flood, the violence of the Flood, and the earth after the Flood:

> The world before the Flood reasoned that for centuries the laws of nature had been fixed. The recurring seasons had come in their order. Heretofore rain had never fallen; the earth had been watered by a mist or dew....
>
> For seven days after Noah and his family entered the ark, there appeared no sign of the coming storm...but upon the eighth day dark clouds overspread the heavens. There followed the muttering of thunder and the flash of lightning. Soon large drops of rain began to fall.... Darker and darker grew the heavens, and faster came the falling rain.... Then "the fountains of the great deep" were "broken up, and the windows of heaven were opened." Water appeared to come from the clouds in mighty cataracts. Rivers broke away from their boundaries, and overflowed the valleys. Jets of water burst from the earth with indescribable force throwing massive rocks hundreds of feet into the air, and these, in falling, buried themselves deep in the ground.... As the violence of the storm increased, trees, buildings,

rocks and earth were hurled in every direction.... Satan himself, who was compelled to remain in the midst of the warring elements, feared for his own existence.

The entire surface of the earth was changed after the Flood. A third dreadful curse rested upon it in consequence of sin. As the water began to subside, the hills and mountains were surrounded by a vast, turbid sea. Everywhere were strewn the dead bodies of men and beasts. The Lord would not permit these to remain to decompose and pollute the air, therefore He made of the earth a vast burial ground. A violent wind which was caused to blow for the purpose of drying up the waters, moved them with great force, in some instances even carrying away the tops of the mountains and heaping up trees, rocks, and earth above the bodies of the dead. By the same means the silver and gold, the choice wood and precious stones, which had enriched and adorned the world before the Flood, and which the inhabitants had idolized, were concealed from the sight and search of men, the violent action of the waters piling earth and rocks upon these treasures, and in some cases even forming mountains above them.[1]

---

1   Ellen G. White, *Patriarchs and Prophets,* Boise, Idaho: Pacific Press Publishing Association, 1958, pp.96-97; 107–108.

About the Author

Emerson A. Cooper is a graduate of Oakwood College (B.A.), the Polytechnic Institute of Brooklyn (M.S. in Chemistry), and Michigan State University (Ph.D.). For forty-four years he has taught chemistry at a small liberal arts Christian college.

During his long and distinguished career as a scientist-educator and a college administrator, he has been the recipient of many distinctive accolades including the following: The First White House Initiative Faculty Award for Excellence in Science and Technology (1988), a resolution passed by the House of Representatives of the state of Alabama honoring him for his outstanding services to Oakwood College (1993), the 1986 prestigious TENNECO-UNCF-Excellence in Teaching Award, the Alabama Association of College Administrators Exemplary Service Award, and Distinguished Leadership Award.

Emerson A. Cooper is also the author of the following two books: *The Core of General Chemistry*, and *To the Unknown God: The God of Science and the Bible.*

Index

To order additional copies of

The **ORIGIN** of the
UNIVERSE

Have your credit card ready and call:

1-877-421-READ (7323)

or please visit our web site at
www.pleasantword.com

Also available at: www.amazon.com